11/26/16

To Juanita
My dear friend
Thanks for wanting to
"pick this up!"
Love,
Harriet

Come September—a Different Kind of Memoir

I Just Said, Oh?

HARRIET A. ROBINSON

WESTBOW
PRESS®
A DIVISION OF THOMAS NELSON
& ZONDERVAN

THE HOLY BIBLE, NEW INTERNATIONAL VERSION®,
NIV® Copyright © 1973, 1978, 1984, 2110 by Biblica, Inc.®
Used by permission. All rights reserved worldwide.

WestBow Press books may be ordered through booksellers or by contacting:

WestBow Press
A Division of Thomas Nelson & Zondervan
1663 Liberty Drive
Bloomington, IN 47403
www.westbowpress.com
1 (866) 928-1240

This book is a work of non-fiction. Unless otherwise noted, the author
and the publisher make no explicit guarantees as to the accuracy of
the information contained in this book and in some cases, names of
people and places have been altered to protect their privacy.

ISBN: 978-1-5127-5305-9 (sc)
ISBN: 978-1-5127-5306-6 (hc)
ISBN: 978-1-5127-5304-2 (e)

Library of Congress Control Number: 2016913394

Print information available on the last page.

WestBow Press rev. date: 09/20/2016

Contents

SECTION 4
Expressions of Introspection

SECTION 5
Expressions of Pain and Contemplation

Preface

It was late June 1937. School was out for the summer, and Mama and I were walking to the grocery store. There she met one of her friends, who stopped to chat. Mrs. Parks nodded an acknowledgment to me, saying, "How old are you now, Harriet?"

"*Seven*," I replied without hesitation.

Mama looked at me strangely, shook her head, and continued chatting. When we returned home, she said, "Harriet, why did you tell Mrs. Parks you were seven when you're only six?"

"Don't you know, Mama?" I said. "I'm not in school in the summer, and I'll be seven come September when school starts again. My bestest friend, Celie—you know how smart she is—well, we had a conversation, and she said how old you are only counts when you're in school!

"And what did you add to this *conversation*?" Mama asked, stressing the word.

Shrugging my shoulders, I answered, "I just said, '*Oh?*'"

Well, come September, in the school of life, I'll still be having conversations, some in fantasy, most in reality. Here, in this book is a representation of the journey so far—poems, plays, stories, and essays of believing, imagining, seeking, despairing, hoping. And saying "*Oh*" whenever a light goes on for me!

I call these writings "a different kind of memoir" because they contain more than memoir. My experiences lead the way, but my imagination breaks loose sometimes. All in all, reader friends, I hope you'll enjoy the book and that from time to time as you read, you'll say "*Oh?*" just as I do!

SECTION I

Expressions of Hope

And hope does not put us to shame because God's love has been poured into our hearts through the Holy Spirit, who has been given to us.
(Romans 5:5 NIV)

I really don't remember when I wrote "Stories in My Head." When I found this poem among my treasures, there was no date on it—just my name and a picture of me at about age seven. In the poem, I suggest that I'll write ten books in my lifetime. Oh?

Stories in My Head

My m'dear tells me that the book she reads to me each night
Were written by some people who put the words down right.
I thought I'd like to make a book; there are stories in my head,
So last night after supper, before I went to bed
I sat down at the table with some paper that I'd found
And thought up a good story and tried to write it down.

Now I can think and I can talk and I read lots of words,
But when I tried to write my book, the words were just like birds!
They flew away each time I tried to put them on the page;
They would not sit upon my pen—*I'm almost in a rage!*

There are so many words I know, but though I frown and frown,
And 'though I try and try and try, I cannot write them down!
My m'dear says that I will learn; my paw-paw says so too,
They say that when I go to school, I'll know just what to do!
I guess the stories in my head will have to wait till then—
But someday I will write my book—not only one, but ten!

It was my parents who gave me an early start with telling stories. First of all, my mother read to my siblings and me every night, and every once in a while she shared funny stories about the children she taught (in a one-room schoolhouse) before she married. I remember one story in particular.

There was a child in the school who, when asked his name, said it rhythmically. Word got around, and when parents or other visitors came to the school, they would look for this child and ask him his name: "What's your name, little boy?"

He would answer each one politely in his rhythmic way: "My name is Jaw-on Paw-ul." Soon, however, he became annoyed with the question, and after a number of challengers sought him, he'd answer, "My name is Jaw-on Paw-ul and Ah'm tarred (tired) now!"

Good for you, John Paul! And thank you for giving me a story to tell!

One of my mother's favorite things to do when we were growing up was to read poetry at high teas that the churches in our neighborhood sponsored. She was always in demand, and she dragged us with her. I don't know about the others, but though I enjoyed mother's readings (and the cookies) at these teas, I didn't enjoy the rest of the program—too long!

My father instituted an activity where the family read the Sunday newspaper together. "Okay, get down on the floor and choose the part of the paper you want to read," he would say. Each of us chose the funnies, of course—and the poetry section that we'd grown to love—before arranging ourselves on the floor, with one stipulation from Daddy: no one's backside could be higher than his head!

Janey Jumps the Broom

Have you ever had the opportunity to visit a slave plantation? Such an opportunity was the highlight of a weekend I spent as a guest at the family reunion of one of my dearest friends. The plantation consisted of a very small slave quarters house and a bit bigger (but not mansion size) plantation owner's house. There was a small cotton field and a small burial ground not very far away from the house.

Years ago, when I had the opportunity to introduce black history to a predominantly white community, a skit about a fictionalized jumping the broom ceremony on a slave plantation came to mind. *Janey Jumps the Broom* is a slight rewriting of that skit

The tradition of jumping the broom is said to have started in Africa to symbolize a new life—letting wearisome things go. Whether slaves in America did it, I don't know, but some African American couples do enjoy celebrating the tradition. When my daughter and son-in-law married nearly ten years ago, they jumped the broom at the reception we had in our backyard. And so, welcome to wherever. Today in my imagination, Janey-Jane Hayes and Stone Barr jump the broom!

Characters
Janey Jane, *the bride*
Mary, *Janey's younger sister*
Sallie Mae, *a neighbor*
Junior, *Sallie Mae's brother*
M'lady, *Janey's mother*
Daddy Herbie, *Janey's father*
Brother Steven, *oldest member of the slave quarter*

Stone Barr, *the groom*
Miss Louella, *a neighbor*
Ruby Ann, *Miss Louella's daughter*
Miss Gloria, *a neighbor*
Ray Becka, *Miss Gloria's daughter*
Wedding guests, *guests and choir*

Scene 1

As scene opens, Janey is painstakingly working on a quilt. She is wearing a sack dress with a rope tied around her waist and a brightly colored bandana. One of her younger sisters, Mary, comes in with friends Sallie Mae and Junior.

Mary: Whatcha doin', Janey?

Janey: You can see what I'm doin', Mary. I'm working on the quilt for my wedding bed. I'm so happy! I'm so lucky! I'm gonna jump the broom with my Stone Barr. (*Sings*) I'm gonna jump with my Stone Barr. I'm gonna jump with my Stone Barr. I'm gonna jump with my Stone Barr, oh yes, oh yes, oh yes! (*She puts the quilt on the chair and twirls around, Mary giggling at her.*)

Mary: Yep! Everybody talkin' about you supposed to jump the broom with Stone Barr on Sunday, but I been wondering how you gonna jump with him, Janey? He a free man, and you a slave.

Janey (*laughing as she sits on the floor*): Oh, Massah, say it's all right. And you know we all going to be free one day. I know that sure as I'm born.

Sallie Mae: You *know* that?

Janey: I know that! I been a-dreamin' about things … and Mary, Massah say I can even go live with Stone Barr in his cabin. I'm gonna have my own cabin, Mary, and my own pallet. Don't have to sleep on the floor no more in this house (*points to the old blanket rolled up on the floor*).

Sallie Mae: Can me and Junior fancy up the broom for you, Janey?

Janey: Sure can, Sallie Mae. I know you'll fix it up real pretty. You come get it next Saturday night. M'Lady will give it to you.

Sallie Mae: Oh, yes, Miss Janey. I never been to a jumpin' the broom, you know. You my first one, and I'm so excited, Miss Janey. You and Mr. Stone gonna jump the broom! Lordy, lordy! One day I'm gonna jump the broom, and I want you to come to mine, Miss Janey. Will you? (*Junior interrupts, preventing Janey's answer.*)

Junior: You jump the broom? Ain't never gonna happen!

Sallie Mae: What? Why you little—I'm gonna get you for that! (*Starts to hit Junior.*)

Mary: Oh, leave him be, Sallie Mae. He don't mean nothin'. He just loves you so much he don't want to see you jump the broom with nobody.

Sallie Mae: He *do not* love me so much! He just a pain-in-the-neck little brother. That what he is!

Junior: Nah, nah, nah, nah, nah! Sallie Mae ain't gonna jump no broom. Sallie Mae ain't gonna jump no broom!

Mary: That not nice, Junior. You better be nice to your sister. We all got to love each other, you know. Folks in the big house ain't never gonna love us the way we got to love each other!

Junior (*contrite and nodding yes to Mary, then speaking to Janey*): Miss Janey, we'll make you a pretty broom—Me and Sallie Mae.

Sallie Mae pretty smart for a girl. You're gonna really like it, Miss Janey, and Mr. Stone too.

Janey: I know I will. (*She goes over to hug Sallie Mae and Junior as they leave.*)

Junior and Sallie Mae: Bye, Miss Janey. Bye, Mary. Bye, M'Lady!

All: Bye!

Mary (*putting her head on Janey's knee, looking up at her and talking a little sadly*): I'm gonna miss you, Janey. You and me been here in this house all these years together …

Janey: Silly little sister. Stone Barr just live 'cross the way. I bet I see you all the time same as now—'cept when we workin'. You in the big house and me in the fields.

Mary: Ain't gonna be the same, Janey. Ain't gonna be the same. You be sticking so close to ol' Stone Barr won't even be funny!

Janey: Well, I guess you a little bit right. I'll be sticking close to Stone Barr, sure enough! I do love that man, Mary. He so tall and so handsome! You see him the other day strutting 'round and all the ol' gals looking at him. But he only got eyes for me. He only got eyes for me, little missy, just me. (*She begins working the quilt again.*)

M'lady (*walking over to a small crate where a white dress has been laid and picking it up*): Janey, you ain't got time to be working on this quilt now. You jumpin' the broom next Lord's Day, and your weddin' dress ain't even finished. You got to help me. You know I got my work to do for Massah.

Janey: Oh, Momma, I know. I know. It's just that I ain't so good at sewing nothin', and I want the quilt to be so special for Stone Barr.

Mary: The quilt's pretty, Janey. That Stone better 'preciate it just like it is. It's real pretty, Janey. *(Speaking to M'Lady)* Cain't I help you with the dress, Momma? I'm near as tall as Janey is, though I ain't quite so skinny! *(She laughs and puts her hands on her hips.)*

Janey: You better git away from here, Mary. And stop calling me Janey. You know I been using my grown-up name. I'm Janey Jane now. Janey Jane Hayes. And I's gonna be Missus Janey Jane Barr. Don't that sound pretty? Missus Janey Jane Barr.

Mary: It do. But you know ain't nobody gonna call you that. You can be Missus Janey Jane Barr in your own mind if you want to, but everybody still goin' to call you just plain old Janey or Janey Baby, like Daddy Herbie call you. Ain't that right, Momma?

M'lady: It ain't important what nobody call her. She know who she is. She my right smart Janey! *(Turning to Janey)* Now come on over here, girl, and try this dress on so I can turn it up right.

Janey: All right, Momma.

M'Lady *(to Mary)*: And you, missy, run on over to Aunt Mandy's and see if she got some white lace we can put somewhere on this dress.

End of Scene 1. Choir singing and keeping time movement with the well-known tune of "I've Got Peace Like a River."

I've got peace like a river,
I've got peace like a river,
I've got peace like a river in my soul.
I've got peace like a river,
I've got peace like a river,
I've got peace like a river in my soul.

I've got joy like a fountain,
I've got joy like a fountain,
I've got joy like a fountain in my soul,
I've got joy like a fountain,
I've got joy like a fountain,
I've got joy like a fountain in my soul,

I've got love like an ocean,
I've got love like an ocean,
I've got love like an ocean in my soul.
I've got love like an occan,
I've got love like an ocean
I've got love like an ocean in my soul!

Hymn: "I've Got Peace Like a River"
Public Domain

Scene 2: *The Wedding Day* in the yard outside the cabin

Choir (*on stage singing and walking off singing. Janey sitting in a chair in her wedding dress*):

This little light of mine,
I'm gonna let it shine.
This little light of mine,
I'm gonna let it shine.
This little light of mine,
I'm gonna let it shine.
Let it shine, let it shine, let it shine!

Shine all over this old world,
I'm gonna let it shine.
Shine all over this old world,
I'm gonna let it shine.

Shine all over this old world,
I'm gonna let it shine,
Let it shine, let it shine, let it shine!

Let it shine till Jesus come,
I'm gonna let it shine.
Let it shine till Jesus come,
I'm gonna let it shine.
Let it shine till Jesus come,
I'm gonna let it shine,
Let it shine, let it shine, let it shine!

This little light of mine,
I'm gonna let it shine.
This little light of mine,
I'm gonna let it shine.
This little light of mine,
I'm gonna let it shine,
Let it shine, let it shine, let it shine!

Negro spiritual: "This Little Light of Mine"
Public Domain

Janey *(talking to herself):* Lordy, lordy, lordy! Sound like angels singin' just for me today. I know the Lord's light is shinin' on me today. It gonna light up my face—and light up my dress—and it gonna light up my Mistah Stone Barr too. Lordy, lordy, I do love that man! I do. I do!

Mary *(coming into the yard)*: Who you talking to, Janey? What you looking so silly for?

Janey: Oh, Mary, I guess I do look a little bit silly—sittin' here grinnin'—but it seems like I just heard angels singin' to me—singin' about shinin' lights. And that's how I feel today, Mary—like all the light in the world gonna shine on me.

Mary *(shrugging her shoulders):* Don't know about you, Janey.

Janey: And stop calling me Janey! I hate it! *(Both laugh.)*

(M'Lady and two neighbors, Miss Louella and Miss Gloria, and their children, Ray Becka and Ruby Ann, come into the yard bringing pots of food.)

Janey: Howdy, Miss Louella. Howdy, Miss Gloria. Hey, Ray Becka. Hey, Ruby Ann. *(Turning to M'Lady)* Momma, what you got in them pots? And *(turning toward Miss Gloria and Miss Louella)*—just look at you—all dressed up in your bestest. Just to see me jump the broom! *(She giggles.)* I'm so excited!

Miss Louella: Howdy, Janey—I mean, Janey Jane. Us too. We been cookin' all week. More food's out there in the creek keepin' fresh.

Miss Gloria: And look at those chillun! *(Pointing to an unseen rotisserie and unseen children)* Over there turning the spit cooking the meat. And you know what we got, Janey—venison. My man got lucky and got a deer last week. How do you like that?

Janey: I like that. Yep, Miss Gloria. I like that. And Stone Barr gonna like that too!

Miss Louella: Stone Barr gonna like anything you like, that's for sure. *(Everybody laughs.)*

Ray Becka: Why you didn't let me work on the spit, Momma? I'm big as Jim Bob and Suzie.

Miss Gloria: No, you ain't, Ray Becka. And you know how you is. You'd start playing with the fire. Don't go on so! There'll be somethin' for you to do.

Ray Becka: (*pouting*), Okay, Momma.

Janey: Come here, Ray Becka. Gimme a hug! You so pretty, and so good.

Ray Becka: You think so, Miss Janey? That's sure somethin'! And I want to grow up to be just like you, Miss Janey.

Sallie Mae *(entering with Junior carrying a decorated broom):* Here's your broom, Janey. I told you we'd make it nice.

Junior: And see that fancy ribbon I tied at the top. I found that in some stuff the Missus threw out. Ain't it pretty?

Ruby Ann *(coming up in front of Sallie Mae):* And don't forget, I gave you the pretty cloth to wrap around it, didn't I, Momma?

Miss Louella: Yes, you did, Ruby Ann. That cloth from the dress from my own momma's jumpin' the broom. We done saved it all this time.

Ruby Ann: That was from Grandma Marilyn's dress? Did Grandma Marilyn look pretty in it? Did Grandpa say he liked it? Did Missus and Massah come to their jumpin' the broom?

Miss Louella: Ruby Ann, stop askin' so many questions! These chillun! Cain't never know when to stop doin' somethin'!

Janey: Oh, everything's all right, Miss Louella. And all y'all—Sallie Mae, Junior, Ruby Ann. It's the bestest broom ever a girl could jump. You all's so good! *(Sallie Mae, Junior, and Ruby Ann smile and curtsey to Janey.)*

Choir (*as wedding guests coming into the yard singing, Mary, Sallie Mae, Junior, among them*):

Is there anybody here who loves my Jesus?
Anybody here who loves the Lord?
I want to know, if you love my Jesus,
I want to know if you love the Lord!

Negro Spiritual: "Is There Anybody Here Who Loves My Jesus?"
Public Domain

Janey (*interrupting the singing to sing by herself*): Yes, there's somebody here who loves King Jesus, somebody here who loves her Lord. And Stone Barr too. Yes, Stone Barr too. I love my Stoney!

Choir (*laughing before resuming the song*):

Makes our souls feel happy when we love our Jesus,
Soul feel happy when we love our Lord!
I want to know, I want to know,
Do you love our Lord?

Stone (*coming into the yard, singing*): Oh, there's somebody here who loves King Jesus. Somebody here who loves my Lord. And Janey Jane too, yes, Janey Jane too. Gonna make her my wife! (*Everyone laughs as Stone goes over and hugs Janey.*)

M'Lady: (*stepping into the yard*) Look like everybody here! Daddy Herbie. You and Brother Steven ready?

Daddy Herbie and Brother Steven: We ready! (*Daddy Herbie speaking to the congregation.*) We is gathered here, my people, to join together my beloved daughter Janey and her beloved friend Stone. Brother Steven, please lead us as we look to the Lord—and make it short, Brother Steve, make it short!

Brother Steven (*giving Herbie a smart look, then looking up and lifting his hands*): Oh, Lord, we thank you this afternoon for these two young folks. We know you have your hand on them, and we know they gonna serve you. Amen. Janey, say yes if that's true.

Janey: Yes, sir, it's true, Brother Steven. It's true!

Brother Steven: Stone, say yes if that's true!

Stone: I am honored to serve my Lord, Brother Steven.

Brother Steven: You all goin' to be the best couple in the quarters. And you goin' raise lots of chillun to make us proud.

Stone: I hope so, Brother Steven.

Brother Steven: Praise the Lord. And now, Herbie gonna pray for his chillun. Bless him, Lord, as he come before us. Bless him, Lord.

Daddy Herbie (*sermonizing*): Oh, Lord, you have heard these chillun's promise to you. Now help 'em to make long, long, long promises to each other. Lord, you know each of 'em—now, Janey—now, Stone—they just a dry bone in the desert without you. But with you, O Lord, flesh covers them dry bones and you puts breath in them. And they is made over in your image, O God. Now reach down, O God, and touch 'em with your tender hand of mercy. Heal any diseases in their hearts, O God. Strike fear in their hearts if they do not obey and care for each other. Oh, Lord God, bless 'em and help 'em all their lives. Amen and amen!

Brother Steven: Thank you, Herbie. Thank you. I know the good Lord gonna honor your prayer. And now, as the oldest member in this here quarter, it be my privilege to speak and console this dear daughter Janey and this dear son Stone as they commits theyselfs to each other. Janey, do you promise to love and obey Stone Barr and to help him in the work that God bless him as a free man to do?

Janey: I do, Brother Steven. I do.

Brother Steven: And Stone Barr, do you promise to love and take care of our dear Janey and treat her good all the time?

Stone: I do, Brother Steven. I do.

Brother Steven: Amen and amen! *(Speaking to the entire congregation)* Now all y'all gathered here, let us all bring our hands together and direct our hearts unto the Lord. We goin' say the prayer the Lord done taught us to say. *(Congregation joining him)* Our Father, who are in heaven. Hallow-ed be thy name. Thy kingdom come. Thy will be done on earth as it is in heaven. Give us this day our daily bread. And forgive us our trespasses as we forgive those who trespass against us. Lead us not into temptation but deliver us from evil. For Thine is the kingdom and the power and the glory. Forever and ever and ever and ever! *Aman* an' *aman*!

Now before Janey and Stone jumps the broom, we gonna hear a song from our li'l choir. What you all gonna sing, sweethearts?

Choir member: We gonna sing "Jesus Loves 'em." We made it up just for Miss Janey and Mistah Stone.

Brother Steven: That sounds just fine. We listenin'!

Choir

Jesus loves 'em, this we know,
For the Bible tells us so;
Miss Ja-a-nee and Mistah Stone,
Both to Jesus do belong!
Yes, Jesus loves 'em,

Yes, Jesus loves 'em,
Yes, Jesus loves 'em,
The Bible tells us so!

Jesus loves 'em, this we know,
For the Bible tells us so;
He will make 'em man and wife—
Save 'em from all sin and strife!
Yes, Jesus loves 'em,
Yes, Jesus loves 'em,
Yes, Jesus loves 'em,
The Bible tells us so!

Altered text sung to the tune of hymn "Jesus Loves Me"
Public domain

Brother Steven: Mighty fine, little gals. Mighty fine! (*The choir smiles and rejoins the guests. Steven speaks to Herbie.*) All right, Herbie, come on over here now and lay the broom before this darlin' couple. Your precious daughter Janey and her spankin' brand new husband Stone. Bless 'em both, Lord, as they does this significance!

Daddy Herbie (*going over to the broom and picking it up, he prays again*): Oh, Lord, before Janey and Stone jump this broom, just take your righteous broom and sweep the corners of their hearts! (*Stopping the prayer to speak directly to Brother Steven*) Brother Steven, can I say one more word to Janey and Stone?

Brother Steven: Sure, Herbie. They your chillun. But keep it short, Herbie—puh-leeze! (*Everybody laughs!*)

Daddy Herbie (*to Steven*): I owes you! (*to Stone and Janey*) Stone and Janey, this broom goin' to sweep away all the ol' crazy stuff from your lives that y'all don't need to keep. Janey, you don't need to keep that stubbiness of yours. Stone, you need to stop thinking about how handsome you is. You a right good-lookin' man! But that ain't all there is to life. (*He lays the broom down in front of the couple.*) You all got to be each for the other and never mind that old stuff you all cares about just for yourselfs. You is now Stone for Janey Baby and Janey Baby for Stone.

Brother Steven: *Aman*, Herbie! *Aman!* *(coughing importantly)* Now with the power give to me because I is the oldest member of this here quarter, I tells you, Stone, and you, Janey, to put your hands together and jump the broom! One, two, three ... *jump!*

Janey and Stone (*as they jump*): I sure do love you, Stone, and I will for the rest of my life ... I loves you with all my heart, Janey!

Brother Steven: Y'all is married! Hallelujah!

Daddy Herbie: Praise the Lord, ever'body! Praise the Lord! (*Everybody claps, and Mary and M'Lady go over to the covered food and begin to uncover it as the curtain closes. The crowd is making its way to Stone and Janey to offer congratulations. One or two people are swaying with the music. Everyone leaves stage while music is still playing.*)

The Other Gold

Is there anything more beautiful than friendship? I don't think so. If I live to be one hundred, I know I'll look forward to calls from my friends—if we still use telephones then. We will moan about the changing world, and we will tell each other about our aches and pains, each striving to outdo the other. And as we hang up, we'll say to each other, "I'm glad you're all right! Good to hear your voice!"

I wrote this piece to express that feeling!

~

Esmay stood on the sidewalk in front of the two-family home she'd lived in for fifty years, resting as always before tackling the four and fourteen steps to her apartment—five cubicles littered with marketplace activity. Her cat watched her from the bay window. She waved and in her lilting "Bajan" accent, called up to him.

"Hey, Pump-kin, how ya be? Be up in a few!"

Reaching the top, she puffed to the soft, old chair in her den. Pumpkin leaped from his padded throne and rubbed against her leg. "Miss me, ya boy?" she said, patting his back, "Me birthday dinner was real good, Mr. Pump-kin. Brought you some, but you gwine wait 'til mornin' … No, nobody go with me, but that's okay. Don't need company to mark time getting' old and crippled up. I am seventy-five today, ya know—and you almost old as me!"

She moistened her lips and coughed to soothe the too-familiar nagging her throat gave when she'd eaten unwittingly. "Real good birthday dinner, did I say, Pump-kin? Yeah." The red eye of her answering machine winked slyly, and she responded as if to an annoying masher. "Leave me be. Leave me be. All these no-count calls." Reluctantly, she pressed play. She frowned as she listened to the messages — one from Agatha Brown in Chicago, the other from Bernice Ashley, who lived just a few minutes away. Slumping forward in her chair, she picked up the cat and reflected on her callers.

Agatha. Dear Agatha. She and Agatha had been friends since they came to the United States from Barbados some sixty years ago, but Esmay held a "little feelin'," as they say, about Agatha. First of all, Agatha had a problem being *Bajan*—spent the first year in the States working day and night to lose the accent. Second, she was bossy. *Give you the shirt off her back if you needed it, but she'd sure tell you how to wear it!* Esmay smiled as she thought about the many times she had "explained" Agatha that way to another acquaintance.

Agatha had visited just last week, leaving George, her husband of forty-four years, to fend for himself for a while. "A misery and a half," she called him. Esmay had long since given up trying to make Agatha see a bright side to the perceived darkness of her marriage.

And Bernice. "Bernice, Bernice," people always said whenever her name was mentioned. Bernice had her ways. She and Esmay didn't visit each other much now; still they had a bond. Esmay was the first person Bernice had met when she'd moved from Virginia to this neighborhood many years ago. They'd enjoyed an intellectual friendship. Bernice was philosophical, and Esmay envied that. Now, as Esmay reflected on their recent conversations, she had to concur that Bernice was becoming, well becoming—her house was bugged, people shouted at her from the television, store monitors followed her every move. Esmay had often tried to joke away her concern when Bernice talked this way. *Ain't neither of us important enough for all that attention, Bernice,* she'd say. *You just got the wannabees!*

Esmay drooped. "I'm too tired," she said, flinging a weary backhand toward the beckoning machine. "I'll call them in the morn-in'." She waddled toward her kitten-sized kitchen, Pumpkin at her heels. After dishing herself a small scoop of ice cream, she called to Pumpkin who had settled himself by the refrigerator, "Time to catch up on me layin' down, Pum-kin. You comin'?"

"Of course," Pumpkin seemed to say as he sashayed toward her. In the bedroom, Esmay turned down the covers and aimlessly searched the TV. Her ears perked as a sarcastic voice from the screen challenged, "I don't let nobody take up residence in my head!" A pudgy man nattily dressed in the gray flannel suit of yesteryear was sounding forth, as a crowd urged him on with hoots and applause.

"Oh, cute!" Esmay said aloud. "Migh-ty cute and clever words! Good for you man! Yes!" But as the camera focused a full head shot on the man, Esmay sensed that he felt neither cute nor clever. *Worried* and *weary* more likely. What had happened to stir some unwanted reality—to make him feel the need to erase someone from his mind? She thought again of Agatha and Bernice as she turned off the TV and settled in for the nightly escape.

Six o'clock, a good hour before her usual waking time, the telephone jerked Esmay awake. "I called you last night," Bernice intoned without waiting for her to speak. "Why'nt you call me back? Just wanted to wish a happy birthday to ya, old friend! How old are you now? Seventy-seven, right? Have you decided to dye that mousy gray hair yet? Gotta look your best, ya know!" Esmay's eyes rolled shut. "And anyway," Bernice continued, "what you doing out so late? It's dangerous out there!"

Quickly, Esmay cut in, her voice syrupy, "Oh hey, Bernice! I was going to call you, but it was past ten when I got in. I thought you'd be long gone sleep. And I'm seventy-*five* for your information!"

"Yeah," Bernice drawled. "Have it your way! Well, anyway,

you know I don't sleep well, and with all the stuff goin' on in this neighborhood, I'm surprised I do at all. Sit here night after night trying to make sense of this old world. Big city living is nothing like back home in Virginia."

Esmay pictured Bernice in her long silk nightgown wearing a blue dangling earring in one ear and chewing on an old fashioned cigarette-less holder. According to Bernice, that blue earring had captured many a brother's fancy in Virginia, and she wasn't going to stop wearing it now.

"And," Bernice interrupted Esmay's thought, "the phone kept ringing—those stupid people trying to get into my business."

"Telemarketers that late at night?" said Esmay.

"Yeah, what they care about what time it is?" Bernice threw her hands in the air.

"They a nuisance factor, all right, Bernice," said Esmay, "but as I told ya, why ya don't get an unlisted number?"

"Can't! You know that! Papi made me promise to keep this number open."

"Papi's gone to his rest, Bernice." The Bajan lilt was gone now. It always went when Esmay was being firm. "I know you'll always want to please him, but he wouldn't want you to be annoyed by an old machine that you can control."

"Well, maybe, I could ..." Bernice's voice trailed off and Esmay thought she heard a tear fall.

"Bernice, Bernice, Bernice," Esmay cried out. "I'm sorry. Didn't mean to make you smart—but you got to excuse me now, dear. I got to run to—you know—just getting up, you know, got to run! Call you this evening. Okay?"

"Okay! Now don't forget! You forget sometimes, you know." Bernice cast a suspicious look at Esmay, who answered sweetly.

"I won't forget, Bernice. I promise." Esmay headed for the

bathroom when the telephone rang again. She picked it up, clenched her free hand and tried to sound cheerful. "Aggie, hi! I was going to call you later ... What's wrong? You're never up this early."

"Oh, nothing. Same old. But I wanted to catch you before you went galloping," Agatha said, her usual impatience evident. "You going to be home this weekend and next week? Can I come for a while?"

Esmay took a breath, but before she could answer, Agatha, voice softer now, started, "Please ..."

Esmay broke in. "I'll be here, Agatha. Yeah, it'll be okay. Come on, I'll meet your flight."

"You're a dear. I'll leave on the shuttle this afternoon. It should be in at seven."

Esmay sat motionless on the bed for a moment, then clasped her hands and bowed her head. "Dear Lord," she prayed, "what more can I do? Say? I pray with her, try to talk her into going for the counseling stuff—even told her to leave the man, and you know I got no right to do that!"

Pumpkin crept from under the bed and sat on Esmay's foot. She continued in prayer. "Lord God Almighty, won't ya help Aggie know you didn't plan for life to be a picnic? George not the perfect man, I know, but Lord, George not all to blame neither. Aggie don't let the man rest—make say about every single thing he do! And she never laugh with him, Father God. And he funny sometimes— makes me laugh anyway." Esmay smiled, a shiver ran through her, and then the tears came. "Yes, Lord, yes. Please. Send someone to help she understand the man! And help she understand she self too, won't you, Lord? You must know some of them folk who can fix up people when they confused. Forgive me, Lord, I didn't mean that like it sounded, but ya got to send someone, Lord, I—I'm tired, and—and—and I feel I'm no use! Thank ya, Lord. Thank ya for what ya gonna do—in the name of Jesus. Amen."

Wiping perspiration from her face, Esmay forced herself to her feet and started to hum, "Ain't going to let nobody turn me 'round, turn me 'round—" The grandfather clock in her living room struck. *Get busy, get busy*, it chimed.

Esmay hadn't picked up her apartment for a while, and even though they were old friends, she didn't want Agatha to see the disarray. Hours ticked by as she whisked through it, challenging herself with every step. Then with just enough time left to get to the airport, she paused. *Just one more thing*, she thought, wiping perspiration—*the front stairs.*

As she rushed to the back hallway to get her dust mop, her right foot cramped, she twisted her back and fell. Slowly she got to her feet, every move a misery. "Oooh," she moaned. *This is all I need.* She let the mop fall and struggled down the stairs and out to her car.

Stalled traffic and slow, painful driving delayed her arrival at the baggage claim area, where Agatha waited. Dressed in high-water slacks and a parka that emphasized her bulk, Agatha paced aimlessly. As Esmay limped to meet her, Agatha, hands on hips, nagged, "Why ya so late?"

"Oh, now, don't ya start with me, Aggie. Just please, come go. I'll tell you about it in the car."

As they turned the corner to descend Esmay's dead-end street, they could see someone sitting on the porch. It was Bernice, her tall, thin frame clothed in a business suit, her wispy gray hair freshly colored.

"It's about time you got here, Miss Esmay," Bernice said as Esmay and Agatha stepped out of the car. "And who's this with you? I told you I'd be here tonight. You have some nerve going out when you knew I was coming."

Stunned, Esmay stammered, "But Bernice, you didn't—I didn't—I told you I'd call you tonight—and I was going to as soon as Aggie and I got settled in. You remember Agatha Brown, don't you? You and I stayed with her in Chicago years ago. She and George were celebrating their twenty-fifth anniversary."

"Hello, Bernice," Agatha said, moving up to the steps. "I remember you. And Esmay mentions you sometimes when we talk. How are you?"

"Oh, so Esmay talks about me, does she?" Bernice fingered her signature earring and moved closer to Agatha. "What did she tell you—she talks too much sometimes!

"N-n-no," Agatha stuttered, avoiding Bernice's gaze as she stepped away from the threat. "She didn't say anything unusual."

"Esmay thinks I don't know what people say about me. Odd, they say. Calling somebody that when all somebody wants is for people on TV to stop bothering her. I'm tired of being the nicety, nice gal all the time. I'm going to get anybody who tries to cross me. And that means you, too, Miss—what did you say your name was?"

"Agatha. Agatha Brown ..." Agatha, said, a bit uncomfortably. Bernice sneered.

What is she going to do? Esmay hobbled up to the deck. *I've got to get between then. I've never seen her like this ...* "Bernice, honey," she said, trying to take Bernice's hand.

"Don't Bernice honey me, you snake," Bernice shouted, pulling out of Esmay's reach. "All hunky-dory with this woman and treating me like dirt! And yeah, Esmay, I think I do remember this woman in Chicago. She was yelling at a man at the party. That was her husband? She didn't act like she even liked him, let alone loved him. Twenty-fifth anniversary? Humph! I can't see those two staying together twenty-five minutes!" She stepped down to the sidewalk, and then, of a sudden, deep sobs racked her body. Agatha stepped down and planted herself directly in front of Bernice, seeming to cover even her shadow.

Esmay reached out. "Don't touch her," Agatha whispered. "Leave it to me. Remember I cared for Mother. I've seen this before."

Then still avoiding Bernice's eyes even as she winced at her remarks, she said, "Please let's go inside and make some tea, Bernice. You and I've got some catching up to do. It's been a long time. And you look great! How do you manage to keep your weight down? I'm forever trying. And your earring! I love it! That's the style the young folks wear. My husband used to say I should be more stylish. He'd really appreciate you!"

"You look okay," Bernice said through tears, "but if you got the next size clothes, maybe you'd look a little better. And if your jacket was black instead of yellow, you wouldn't look so fat!"

A gasp slipped from Esmay's mouth. *How was Agatha taking this?*

"And Bernice," Agatha continued unflinchingly, "I know Esmay's really sorry she wasn't able to call you earlier. It's my fault. I called and told her I had no way of getting here from the airport and she rushed down—please forgive her. She's such a friend to both of us; I'd hate to see her unhappy because of something I'd done."

Bernice stared at Agatha. Agatha met her gaze, and neither spoke for a moment. Then, to Esmay she growled, "Where's her bag?"

"I'll get it." Esmay, fearful now, walked toward her car, as Bernice and Agatha remained motionless.

"What did you say your name was again?" Bernice held out her hand to Agatha.

"Agatha."

Bernice looked into Agatha's eyes. "Agatha. Agatha. Papi would like that name." She put her hand to her face and nodded. "You're right, Miss Agatha. Esmay is a good friend. But she's changed. She doesn't come to my house anymore, and every time I call her, she's busy. And you know what else? When I tell her something, I know that she doesn't believe me." She crossed her arms dramatically. "But she doesn't know what happens in my house. She's not there."

"That's true," Agatha said. "She's not."

Esmay had been standing on the sidewalk with Agatha's bag. "Let's go up," she said. The three marched penguin file to Esmay's apartment. Pumpkin met them at the top of the stairs.

"Hi Pump-kin," Agatha said. "Tell your mother here to get out the fancy china and make like we're special!"

"Good idea, Aggie," Esmay said. "Chicken wings and potato chips look great on fancy china. I'll make a plate for you, too, cat."

Bernice walked gingerly around the cat. Pumpkin peered at her suspiciously and scampered off. "And don't forget the tea cups, Esmay dear," she called as Esmay left for the kitchen. "Agatha's going to make me some Earl Grey tea—my favorite, you know. Hope you have some." She went to the hall closet where Esmay kept her old TV trays and took out three of them. "I'm getting the trays for us. Not to worry. Just bring a rag so I can dust them. They're awful dirty!

This is so odd, Esmay thought as she took some cooked chicken wings from the freezer and turned on the oven. She thought of her many dismal conversations with Agatha and worrisome confrontations with Bernice. *I'm actually enjoying myself*, she said almost aloud. *They're weird, but they're fun.*

From the living room, Bernice interrupted Esmay's thoughts. "Hey dear," she called. "I think I'll spend the night. Papi doesn't like me coming in after seven o'clock, and here it is seven fifteen already."

Esmay ignored the comment. "Food'll be ready in a few minutes," she said, laughing. "Come and get it in about fifteen."

"Okay," Agatha and Bernice said in duet.

On their way back to the living room, Bernice sidled up to Esmay. "Did you hear what I said? *I've got to spend the night* because it's later than when Papi wants me home!"

"Bernice, your father's gone!"

"Esmay! I know Papi's dead!" Bernice shouted. "I'm not crazy, okay?"

"Umm, umm," Agatha coughed.

The three set their plates down on the living room table. "No, I know you're not. Sure, sure stay, Bernice. If you don't mind the couch, sure," Esmay said.

On Sunday morning, the comforting aroma of fresh coffee awakened Esmay. She glanced over to the far side of her king-size bed where Agatha had slept and called, "What's going on out there?"

"Pre breakfast in bed for you," said Agatha, appearing with a small tray of toast and coffee. "Stay in bed for a while and rest your back. I'll fix a real breakfast. Then I'll wake Bernice."

Bernice shouted at them through the bathroom door. "I'm in here. Be right out. I've got something to show you."

"You did this whole puzzle this morning? And in ink, too?" Agatha exclaimed as she surveyed the *New Yorker* magazine Bernice proudly displayed when she emerged from the bathroom. "Sometimes I can do the one in my neighborhood paper, but the *New Yorker*? Oh my socks and shoes! And in ink, too!

"What's with this 'in ink, too' business you're getting so excited about?" Bernice said, giving Agatha a look that would have withered an apple on a cold day in January. "When Esmay talks about me, doesn't she tell you that I'm smart?"

"Hey gals," Esmay interrupted, "come on, let's eat." Soon the three were savoring Spanish omelets, bacon, and grits.

Bernice stood up. "Hey, you two," she said. "Do I look a scream in this big flannel nighty Esmay gave me last night? I never wear *flannel* nighties—just silk!" Demurely Agatha put her hand to her own too-small pajama top and closed a gaping buttonhole. She shifted her eyes from Bernice to Esmay and too loudly said, "And I'll bet you look great in them, too!"

"I'll bet she does. Bernice always looks nice," Esmay said cautiously. Bernice stood up and wheeled around, the grand dame in a fabulous fashion show. Agatha sought Esmay's eyes, searching for a hint of fear.

"You know what George would say about us enjoying ourselves like this?" said Agatha.

"That women are crazy!" Bernice said.

Agatha laughed. "Yup, every time I go out with a couple of friends, he's got to say, 'I wish I knew what you all see in each other. You women are crazy!'"

"And we are!" Esmay laughed. "Ever notice how when we go out we even go to the ladies' room together?"

"Yeah, we do, don't we! But is that his business? How much time does he spend with me?" Agatha shrugged.

"You told me he took you and a couple of friends out for your birthday," Esmay said.

Agatha rolled her eyes. "Humph! Yeah, you're right, he did— and my birthday was exactly eleven months ago tomorrow!"

Bernice put her empty plate on the table and turned to Agatha. "What you getting bent out of shape for, Missy? Your husband's probably no worse than mine was—rest his soul. Just don't depend on him to be your friend. That's what Papi used to tell me."

"Make sure you keep girlfriends, huh, Bernice," Esmay said.

"Yeah, that's what Papi said—but only if they're gold. Can't trust the silver ones!"

Bernice looked sad for a moment. Esmay looked at Bernice

and pursed her lips. She wanted to say, "What in the world are you talking about?" but better judgment caused her to ask, "What do you mean, Bernice?"

"You don't know that old saying, Esmay? You been under a rock? *'Make new friends, but keep the old. One is silver and the other gold.'* Trouble is, silver tarnishes. I don't want me no silver friends!"

"Well," said Esmay, "that's true. Silver does tarnish, but it's as good as new when you polish it. New friends can be really special."

"Oh, Esmay, you're always full of that philosophical stuff. You don't know so much," said Bernice. "And there's another thing *I* know you don't know!"

"What?" asked Esmay, more curious than annoyed.

"You don't know about husbands. Now me, I know about husbands." Looking straight at Agatha in her too-small pajamas, Bernice continued. "I know husbands don't like ugly night clothes, and I know husbands don't like wives who don't pay them no mind. Maybe you don't pay him mind enough!"

Agatha flushed and drummed on her lap. "George is not—and Bernice, you don't even know my husband, so …"

Smack! Agatha fell back from Bernice's blow, and Esmay started up from her lounging position—too quickly for her sore back. Her head hit the corner of the table. Blood gushed, and she fell.

"See what you've done," Bernice shouted. "It's all your fault— you—Miss *A-ga-that*!"

"Bernice," Agatha cried, "shut up! Help me get Esmay up! We'll have to get her to the hospital. Get some ice and put it in a towel. I'll drive and you'll sit in the back and hold the ice to Esmay's head."

"That, I think, will be a good thing to do," said Bernice. "You drive and I'll tend to Esmay."

A smile forced its way through Esmay's pain. Here was the

Agatha she knew of old—unselfish, feisty, caring, not whining and complaining.

"Eyegatha," Esmay whispered in a pronounced Bajan accent when Bernice left to get ice. "Ya t'ink ya can come back in a time or two and we take up with Bernice? I t'ink she might listen to ya and get some doctor help!"

"She might at that," Agatha said, and then in the lilt of her own long-ago past, she added, "Mmm—mebee me ask me George to come wit' me. He seem to have a calmin' effect on folk—'ceptin' me." She lowered her head shyly. "But—mebee. Mebee him and me could stay in that new little hotel ya told me about …"

Esmay reached for Agatha's hand. "Mebee," she said.

Martin Luther King Jr. Wants Us to Tell 'Em

"Tell 'em I tried to love somebody," this modern prophet said.
"Tell 'em I tried to keep somebody from losing heart and head.
Tell 'em I tried to lift 'em up—not black, not white, but all.
Tell 'em I heard the Master's voice, tell 'em I heeded His call.
Tell 'em they've got to keep on striving, keep up a noble fight;
Tell 'em it never will be easy, but it always will be right!
Tell 'em it's really up to them to help this world along,
Tell 'em to hold each other's hands and sing a hopeful song!
Tell 'em to try to love somebody when they are most afraid—
Tell 'em to try to help somebody to use both heart and head.
Tell 'em to lift the people up—not black, not white, but all!
Tell 'em to heed the Master's voice. Tell 'em to *seek His call*!"

~

Martin Luther King Jr. lost his life but shared his dignity and immeasurable contribution to America with the world. Everyone did not embrace him, but there were some who thought he should be awarded the Nobel Peace Prize for his work—the rest, as they say, is history!

I met Dr. King on two occasions—when at age twenty-seven, he was the main speaker at my graduation from college, and years later when he knocked on my parents' door in Dorchester during a visit to the African American community of our city "just to chat a minute," he said. As we filed out of the commencement exercises,

Rev. King shook my hand as he did all the graduates, but I felt so special! And our entire community felt pretty special when he visited our homes "just to chat."

And then came April 5, 1968, the day after his assassination. I went to work that day—the only person of color in my job. When I arrived at the office, no one looked my way. No one spoke to me. Most heads were bowed, solemnity that I had never seen before. The next day, my superior (that's what we called bosses back then) asked me if I would write an article about Dr. King. Would I? It was published in one of our textbooks. Then years later on one of the anniversaries of Martin Luther King Day, I wrote the poem you just read, hoping to share it, hoping that all of us would be reminded of our forever task!

SECTION 2

Expressions of Wonder

Even small children are known by their actions, so is their conduct really pure and upright? Ears that hear and eyes that see—the Lord hath made them both. (Proverbs 20:10–11 NIV)

Our Four Boys

Mischief is as mischief does—
Crash! Bang! Wham! Buzz, buzz, and buzz!
Into this and into that—
Oops, there goes Ma's Sunday hat.
Quietness is something rare.
Duck! Ray's going to throw that chair.
Watch out, Jackie's gone to get him,
Screaming because Wayne won't let him!
What now? Hear little Donald's squall.
They're our four boys—we love 'em all!

There's a horse in our front room,
Least that's what they call our broom.
Takes 'em lots of places too,
Last week it was Kalamazoo.
No telling where they'll go today!
They may wind up in Santa Fe,
Ghana—perhaps a British Isle;
Wherever they go, they'll make 'em smile
And captivate the hearts of all who see.
Our four boys—so bright, so free!

Though our four boys are mischief makers,
They really are quite nice;
And if we had a chance to trade 'em,
We'd think about it twice.
And then perhaps a million more—
'Midst smiles and tears—a bump, a fall;
They're our four boys. We love 'em all!

~

"Our Four Boys" is written in honor of the first four of my nephews. They were all that I had for a while, and they were delightful. I dedicate this poem to them and to all the nephews and nieces, grandnieces (niecelets), grandnephews (nephewlets), greater grands, cousins, godchildren, and children of close friends who call me Auntie. They're my family—and I love 'em all!

Choosing

"I'm happiest when I can choose
First one thing then another;
Some things I like,
And some I don't,"
Said Barry to his brother.
"I chose today
To read a book,
I chose to walk the dog.
I didn't choose
To jump around
Like a silly little frog!
Do you know why I like to choose?
It tells me how I feel;
If I choose this instead of that,
I'm being *me*—
for real!"

A Note to Children

Long time ago, folks used to say
Children should be seen, not heard.
That meant that youngsters—boys and girls—
Would utter not a word
Until they were asked a question!
Then they'd answer pure and sweet,
And never pout, or move about,
Or stamp their little feet!

Today, it's rather different.
Children clamor for their space
And pay no attention to what's said
By adults who are in the place
In which they are standing,
Or sitting, or slumping in their chairs!
Or—chewing gum so madly,
The sound hurts a body's ears!
Now, God did not intend
That children should be seen, not heard—
He wants to hear their questions,
Know their feelings, trust their words.

For children have quite much to say,
And adults should surely listen
When children's speech and actions show
That they, too, have a mission
To learn, to love, even to teach—
To be the best that they can be,

To make the world a better place
For themselves, for you, for me!

So children, be what God intends;
Don't clamor for your space.
Polite behavior still means much
In this world and in this place.
Try hard to pay attention
To things said or done for good,
And say a "please" and "thank you"
Whenever you know you should!

"Good morning" or "good evening"
When people pass your way
May help someone who feels alone
To have a better day.
But best of all, politeness will make *you* feel so good
You'll wonder why you waited—
You'll feel *you're* understood!
God bless you!

A Child Thinks about His-Story

I celebrate two histories—
One black, the other white.
Without both, I can't imagine
What my life would be like!

My black history tells me that
Some of my ancestors were stolen
From their home in Africa
To become slaves in North America,
And that they suffered a lot.

My black history also tells me
That even though our people were slaves,
They're great people!
And that's true, I know.
Look at my dad!

My white history tells me that some of my ancestors
Came to America from Italy to have a better life.
They were very, very poor.
They had some bad times in Italy
And had to work very, very hard.

My white history also tells me
That even though my people had some bad times
And they were very, very poor
And had to work very, very hard,

They're great people!
And that's true, I know—
Look at my mom!

Both my histories tell me that some of my ancestors
Were kings—
And queens—
And princes—
And princesses!

That may be why Dad and Mom
Sometimes call me prince—
And call my sister princess!

Would you like to be a princess or a prince?
Well, just celebrate your histories,
Whatever they may be;
Honor God in all you do,
Do good for folks for free—
And you will wear the shiniest crown
The world will ever see!

The Day Love Was Born

I was nine years old when the great hurricane of 1938 hit New England. As memory serves me, my older brother had been playing outside in the balmy weather that often precedes a bad storm, but now he was nowhere to be found! I remember Mama's worrying and scolding when he appeared all smiles, saying, "It's such a beyootiful day!"

Years later, as a full-grown adult and the parent of a teenager, Mama shared this tidbit with me: "When you all were teenagers, I went to the church every day—church doors were open every day then—to pray for God to keep you safe and keep you doing right!

As I think about other adult conversations I've had with both my parents, friends, and even children, I'm jarred into realizing that we certainly could have been perpetrators of the pain, frustration, and worry that parenthood brings! And as I look back, my imagination tingles. The story you are about to read was not one of my parents' experiences, but well, if you've ever been a parent ...

~

"Clarence! Cla-a-a-rence! Last time I'm calling you, boy! Come get to these dishes!"

Louise Hawley's usual lilt was raspy. In her seventh month of pregnancy, she wearied of her heavy body and of caring almost single-handedly for her thirteen-year-old son.

She plopped down on a rickety wooden chair in the kitchen of her four-room tenement apartment. So abrupt was her descent that her worn and faded plaid dress split. She leaned into her hands, tears in her eyes, "Cla–a-rence," she moaned, her voice growing stronger. "*Now!*"

Clarence strolled into the kitchen, clothes limp on his thin, slightly bent frame. He grinned as if for a toothpaste ad. "Hi, Mama," he said. "I thought I heard you call me. Did you?"

"Yes, Clarence, I call you," she said, the Bajan thrust of her childhood creeping into her voice. "I call and call you! You know you have dishes to do!"

"Mama," he said, still smiling. "I made a house out of one single piece of wire, and I didn't even have to use more wire. Do you want to see it?"

"No, I do not," Louise replied. "You always tinkerin' 'round with something!"

"Okay," he said, shrugging. He spun across the room to clear the table. Louise shot him a look; he stopped twirling and stared at her. "You know I don't like to do dishes, Mama. Anyway, why didn't you and Daddy do them? Daddy told me you would."

"Daddy told you what? What?" Louise's breath was coming in spurts. "Not a care do I have what Daddy told you. Do them!"

"Okay! Okay! Mama," Clarence said. He shook his head from side to side and chanted, "The shadow knows, the shadow knows."

Louise raised herself slowly and lumbered to her bedroom. "Plus do the pots!" she called back to Clarence. In her room, her salty tears stung the places around her mouth and chin where she constantly dug for ingrown hairs. "Oh, precious Savior, help me, please," she cried. "I do not like my son! I do not like my son! And he do not like me!"

Clay Hawley, Louise's husband, was a porter on the Boston and Maine Railroad and had two- or three-day breaks at home only seven or eight times a year. He was on a break now and had gone to get the evening paper, unaware that war was waging in his home.

Returning from his walk, the tall, muscular man strode into the kitchen. "Guess who I saw at the store?" He stopped short and grinned at his son. "Hey pal," he said, "What you doing in here? I told you I'd do the dishes."

"Mama's making me do them whether you told her don't or do! She don't like me, you know!" Clarence mimicked his mother's accent and laughed, and then he flicked a little water at his father.

"Not true," said Clay. "Not true. Y'all just have ways about you." He tossed his tweed cap onto the kitchen table and sat down. "And where is your mama? Where's my beautiful wife?"

Clarence shrugged. "In y'all's room, I guess."

Clay turned toward the bedroom. "Something wrong, Lulu," he called.

"Go see," said Clarence.

Clay went into the bedroom and pushed the door open. *Yeah, something's wrong.* Louise was lying face-down on the bed. He stepped over the spread she had thrown at the door and tried to embrace her. She stiffened and pulled away. "Honey, what's the matter?" he asked.

Her dam burst. "It's Clarence. He hate me. I try and I try. Since he a baby, I try," she sobbed.

Clay reached for her again, and she released herself to him. "Louise," he said, "you're just tired. And I know you must be just a little scared! After all, four miscarriages!"

"No," she cried. "It's Clarence. You don't know. He pay me no mind ever! You should hear how many times I call him to the kitchen today!"

"Oh that!" Clay said. "Lou, I told Clarence you and I would do the dishes. I thought we'd make tonight special—do the dishes together, laugh, and throw water at each other. You know, like we used to when we were first married. We had such fun in those days, Lou, didn't we? And tomorrow night, guess what, I'm taking you to see Mary Martin in *My Heart Belongs to Daddy.*" He leaned to hug her.

"Oh Clay," she said, hugging him, her anger subsiding. "But I wish you'd told me about the dishes. I hate myself when I worry at Clarence, but I just can't seem to help it."

"Want to talk about it?" said Clay.

Tears welled again. *How can I tell him how I feel about our son?* "I don't know," she said. "All I know is he does-not-like-me! Even when he's small, he didn't. You know how I always took him places and tried to show him things? He never fun with me like other pinkney. Other children lookin' around asking questions, laughin', talkin' to their mamas! Not Clarence." Then clutching her stomach, she looked coldly at her husband. "I do not want this baby, Clay. I don't want another Clarence!"

"You can't mean that, Louise," Clay said, his eyes bulging. "You been building this up all these years? I know Clarence has some quirks, but he is your pinkney, Lulu. *Our* baby. The only one God has let us have so far. He's just a little boy wanting to have things his own way." Clay's face broke, and he looked so much older than his not-yet-forty years.

"Well, he ain't big enough to carry he own ship to sea." Louise shook her fists. "And he not normal. Remember the doctor told us when he's born, he wish he'd weighed more."

"Louise, he is normal," said Clay. "Whatever that is. And don't forget, I heard that doctor talk too. Seems to me, as they say in your country, the more ya watch, the less ya see!"

Louise trudged on in her determination to get this awful hurt out. "Do all pinkney do phony smiles when their mamas talk to them? Look see Clarence when your sister come 'round. All hugs and talking! And Mrs. Butler across the street—he does anything she wants. Me? I'm lying here tired the other day and ask him for water. Did he come? No!"

"That's little stuff, Louise. Forget it. Forget it," Clay said. His voice was hard. Then, softer, "I'll talk to him—and Lou, it might not be a bad idea for you to talk with Reverend Clark." His voice trailed off in a hoarse whisper as he headed for the kitchen. Louise shook her head sadly.

Warm breezes wafted through the open window the next morning. To Louise they felt like the tropical breezes of Barbados. As she walked into the kitchen, Clarence did so too. "Take your cap off in the house!" she said to him. "And stocking supposed to be under the cuff, not outside the cuff. Here, let me fix you."

Clarence ambled over to his mother, the usual smile playing on his lips, and let her pull up his stocking and straighten his suspenders. "Bye, Mama," he said as he skipped out the door.

Sherwin School, where Clarence attended, was just a few blocks away. It let out at 2:00, but at 3:00, Clarence wasn't home. Like chameleons, the soft breezes of the morning now lashed houses and forced leaves from the trees. *A storm, and a big one, is brewing*, Louise thought. "Clay, get up!" She opened their bedroom door. "I think there's a storm coming, and Clarence isn't home yet."

"He'll get here, Lulu," Clay murmured sleepily and then added mischievously, "but I'm glad to see you're concerned!" He turned over.

"Clay," Louise shouted, "get up! We have to look for Clarence!" She handed him the trousers he had thrown on a chair.

In a moment with the sheeting rain and the wind whipping around them, Clay and Louise struggled down Westminster Alley, where Mrs. James inched the door of number 2 open and shouted, "What's wrong, Mrs. Hawley? I didn't know you were home, Mr. Hawley."

"You seen Clarence?" Louise gasped, her lungs burning. "He's not home from school."

"Haven't seen him," Mrs. James said, "but I'll bet he went to Mrs. Joseph's house when he felt the wind coming."

Yes, that's where he'll be, Louise thought. Tommy Joseph was Clarence's best and only friend, but Louise had never visited the family. It seemed strange to ring their doorbell now.

"Why hello, Mrs. Hawley," said Mrs. Joseph. "Come on in, both of you. You're soaking!"

Trying to hold back her tears, Louise said, "We're looking for Clarence. He here?"

"Goodness me, no dear," Mrs. Joseph said, picking up the edge of her apron to wipe her face. "Even Tommy's not here. Sent him off yesterday to visit his uncle in Connecticut for a week. Boy's been giving me a lot of sass. Needs a man's arm around him, I guess. Since my Thomas died, we've had a time!"

Louise started to cry. "Don't you fear, Mrs. Hawley, Mr. Hawley," Mrs. Joseph said softly. "You'll find him, that's for sure, and he'll be all right!"

Clay took Louise's arm and thanked Mrs. Joseph. "Come on dear," he said to Louise. "We'll go down to Madison Park and look. He likes to go down there, you know." As they began the quarter of a mile walk, no sooner had they reached the edge of the park when they heard the frightened voice of their son. "Somebody help me! Somebody, please!"

"We're here!" shouted Clay, "we're here!"

A few yards into the park, they saw him. He was in a tree, holding onto a massive branch, his knickers dangling from the waist. One shoe had fallen to the ground. The abating winds allowed Clay to lift a long, heavy branch from the tree and direct it toward Clarence. "Slide down the branch, Son," he said.

"Mama," Clarence's voice fluttered down. "I can't. It will hurt, won't it?"

Louise winced. "You have to, Clarence. And you can. Come on, do it for Mama!"

Gingerly Clarence slid down and fell into his mother's waiting arms, causing her to fall. "Clay," she gasped. Clay knelt to pick her up, and the three of them stumbled over to a bench and sat down. As they did so, Louise cried out in pain.

Clarence stroked her stomach. "Don't cry, Mama, don't cry," he said. "Come on, me and Daddy will carry you. We have to get you home, and I'll get the doctor!" Clay lifted Louise, Clarence by his side for the long walk home.

Clay gently laid Louise on the bed. "Clarence," he said, "You and me gonna bring a baby into the world in a minute!

Louise sat up and rocked herself, gasping. She said, "Clay, go boil water and get some clean sheets!"

Clarence rolled his mother from one side of the bed to the other. "Ooh," he said, putting his hands over his eyes. "Mama, Mama, what shall I do?"

"Get your daddy. Tell him to bring the water even if it's not boiling."

Clarence and Clay worked swiftly, and soon, "Waa," a precious cry came forth. As they wrapped the tiny girl in a slightly torn and faded pink towel and presented her to Louise, Clarence asked, "Can we call her Love? L-O-V-E, Love. That's Tommy's sister's name, and she's so nice!"

Clay looked at his wife. Both gazed at Clarence. *His smile is the calm after the storm,* Louise thought as she beckoned to him. "Sure, me pinkney, sure, sure. Love Hawley, me Clarence's own baby sister!" Holding the baby in one arm, she reached for Clay and Clarence with the other and whispered, "Me darlins—de last calf ain't kill the muddah!"

"Praise the Lord," said Clay.

"I love you, Mama," said Clarence.

Something Special Happened to Me Today

True tidbits of special times in my life, written on the day they happened.

June 23, 1981
Budding Genius
My nephew and his wife have been vacationing in Hawaii. Today I received a card from them. It didn't say much, just "thinking about you," but that was enough! My nephew had won that trip in recognition of his budding genius as a businessman. This reminded me of a conversation I had long ago with my sister about her son. While I was working in Virginia at my first *big* job at twenty-one, my nephew was carving his way into his first *big* job at ten. This shy little boy began making potholders with a wooden spool and knocking on doors to try to sell them. *Everybody* needed a potholder! He saved the money he had made and bought packets of seeds; sold them too. *Something special happened to me today!*

May 12, 1982
What Makes a Relative?
Yesterday I had my ears pierced. This morning I am still complaining about the pain. Roberta, my daughter, asked me how my ears felt. I told her that one felt fine, but the other hurt a little. She asked me which one (because one of her ears keeps getting infected). I showed her the right side of my face. "Same as mine," she said, showing me the right side of her face. She then broke into a huge grin. "Oh, that's

why we're related," she said. "You hurt where I hurt." I just hugged her. *Something special happened to me today!*

June 10, 1982
Mind Your Own Business
Walking during my lunch hour, I saw a group of nursery-school age children walking along, obviously on a school outing. Each child was holding a Happy Meal from McDonald's in his (her) outside hand. With the inside hand, each held fast to a partner—all except the last two in the group. These two very short boys were not holding hands, rather they were turning to each other every now and again and laughing and talking with each other, having a very good time. Their lively conversation surprised me—they were so young. What could they be talking about and enjoying so much? I walked up behind them and said, "Aren't you two supposed to be holding hands?" With a look that said, "Who are you and what business is it of yours?" they switched hands for their Happy Meals and held on to each other, with not a look back in my direction. *Something special happened to me today!*

June 24, 1982
Recognizing a Child's Bent
Early this morning, about 7:30, my niece Karen called me to say that Roberta's picture was on the front page of our standard newspaper. "What?" I said. "Why?" (My daughter hadn't told me that she'd had her picture taken. I guess we'd been too busy the night before—always too busy!) When I got to work, a copy of the paper was on my desk. Throughout the day, my phone didn't stop ringing, more copies of the paper were put on my desk, and finally Roberta arrived with her dog-eared copy in hand, so excited—not because *her* picture was in the paper, but because the picture of the children was. "Imagine how they'll feel when they get to be ten

or eleven years old!" she said. She was as excited as I've ever seen her, and I recognized, at last, that she was bending in the way God meant for her to bend. Her love of learning about babies and young children has been evident from birth almost. Parents have begun to trust her completely to babysit responsibly. She is fifteen years old. *Something special happened to me today!*

January 16, 1985
Who's Teaching Whom?
Sitting with Roberta at the kitchen table, we were talking about her friends. She told me that they were always borrowing from her, sometimes without even asking. I told her that she would have to learn to say, "I don't mind lending, but I'd like to be asked." I added that refusing requests was hard to do, but a must if she didn't want to be in the losing seat forever. I told her she'd have to learn how to refuse in a nice way and that was often hard to do. Just this week, I told her. I refused a volunteer job with the church, but I wasn't happy with the way I'd refused. "How would you have done it?" I asked.

She looked thoughtful. "Well," she mused, "I think I'd have said, 'Thank you for the opportunity, but I just don't have the time to do that right now.'"

Wow! Maybe everything that's asked of us *is* an opportunity for us, one way or another. Who advised whom here? And because all has not been going well with us recently, my talk with this provocative, maddening, sensitive, unpredictable young woman made me feel that *something special happened to me today!*

November 11, 1985
Surprise!
Today is a holiday, and there were few people on the subway, perhaps nine or ten in my car. Sitting across from me was a boy

of about thirteen or fourteen reading a book, obviously absorbed in it. Suddenly, he chuckled. A while later, he chuckled again. His unabashed enjoyment of that book emboldened me to get up and sit beside him. "Excuse me," I said "I'm a textbook editor, and I sometimes get to choose books for people your age to read. Would you mind telling me the name of the book you're reading? You really seem to be enjoying it."

He didn't tell me the name right away but started right in telling me the story from the beginning. (He was about halfway through.) "Yes," he said, "this is a good book. I can't believe I'm reading instead of listening to my Walkman. My Walkman is right here in my bag! I have to read this book for a book report, but I really like it. *I* hate *reading* but *this is a good book*! The guy in this story always thinks positive—not negative like I would if I was in an avalanche."

He showed me the cover of the book saying, "See, this is the guy—and you can see his backpack—that's where he's got the raw grouse that he's going to have to eat to survive. Eck! Then he introduced himself. "My name's James. What's yours?" I told him. "Hey," he said, "this is a great way to meet a person!" I thought so too. *Something special happened to me today.*

Sometime in 1938
The Day I Found Out What Was Not To Be My Destiny
Besides my mother's oratory and musical skills, and my father's no-nonsense reasoning and wit, something else happened one day that figures largely in my preoccupation with story. The year was 1938, and I was nine years old. Our small Sunday school staff had planned a stage play. I wanted to try out for the main part, which required a tall child who could lead the "soldiers for the Lord" in a rollicking march down to the river. The child had to be able to sing the spiritual "Down by the Riverside."

A little taller than most of the children, I was a confident contender. Besides the advantage of my height, my Sunday school teachers as well as my regular teachers had always praised me when I read aloud, and secretly I loved to sing. *And so*—in my shiny patent leather Mary Jane shoes and my favorite plaid jumper, I marched up the makeshift steps to the stage and planted myself in the middle of the platform. The other tryouts and the adults in the room applauded when I read my lines. I shivered with joy. Then Miss Simmons, the venerable and feared Sunday school superintendent, said, "Sing!" The pianist played a few introductory notes and I began. "Gonna lay down my burden …" Miss Simmons frowned and pursed her lips. Maybe I wasn't singing loudly enough. I opened my mouth as widely as I could and bellowed, *"Down by the riveride!"* Miss Simmons raised one hand to her forehead and lowered her eyes. Then very slowly, she waved the other hand toward me. "That's fine, dear. You may take your seat."

But I hadn't finished! Didn't she know I hadn't finished? A hush descended upon the room as muffled giggles deafened me. I just stood there, knowing that the part would not be mine.

I don't remember how I got down from the stage or how I got through the next few days. I don't even remember if I got another part in the play. I only knew I had failed. Even worse, I'd failed at something I loved to do.

Eventually I accepted the truth about my singing voice. The teasing I got whenever I sang told me that my voice must have sounded like chalk scraping a blackboard. But singing was in my heart, and its expression could not be stilled. I sang all the time, and even though I wasn't good at singing, it framed the page that was to become my story—that failure is not final! Opportunities abound to reach for the best in others and ourselves. My failure to become a Sunday school thespian is not consciously on my mind when I've set goals, but it serves to remind me that while the defeats of our lives may tell us that we are not singers, we should never embrace as fact that we cannot sing! *Something special happened to me one day in 1938.*

Saturday at Play—I Can't Remember When
I saw a part of the vivid and wonderful world of children one Saturday afternoon. As I sat on a bench by the neighborhood playground, children showed me a sidewalk, a tree, and a little bit of sky.

The cold gray sidewalk with the aid of grubby chalk-laden children quickly became a huge, unordered blackboard, magnificent because there were no teachers to dictate the writing; immensely proportioned checkerboards with little humans portraying the blacks and reds; and hunting grounds for fierce, terrifying jungle animals. The cracks in an ordinary sidewalk are simply small openings in which it's easy to lose a pin or a matchstick, but from the cracks in "Saturday-at-play" sidewalks tiny, tiny trees can and do grow and house the ant-like jungle animals that stalk to and fro with their rations on their backs. And who has not seen a tiger, however small, that was not strikingly orange painted with night-black stripes? In a playground, the world of make believe is intensified a hundred thousand times, and it becomes truly real that a cold, gray sidewalk is a myriad of color and expression.

And have you ever truly seen a tree? Picking me out from the other onlookers, one child called, "Hey, look at the crying tree!" I looked. I *saw* a crying tree. The weeping willow is our common name for it, and anyone who has ever observed one knows that it droops, but how many of us have seen it cry? As it stood sorrowfully by the cool, calm lake, I looked and listened very carefully. I noticed a ripple in the lake and a rustle of the leaves as the breeze hurried through the weeping willow. I thought, yes, a tear has fallen!

Since morning, the sky had been shadowy, the sun peeping through occasionally to see if anyone was around. Now it threatened angrily. It was going to rain! We'd all have to go home! The children ignored the announcement. "It won't rain; we know it won't," they chanted. But it did begin to rain, and in that moment, the beautiful blue and white sky with its flecks of gray and its playful darts of yellow became an ugly, terribly authoritarian blackguard that saddened the trusting children.

Starting for home in the rain was disappointing to their parents, too. They understood the children's unhappiness. But as quickly as the rain came, it stopped. The reluctant and indecisive sky had given the children another chance to play in their wonderful world—and we onlookers stayed a little longer too. *Something special happened to me that day!*

SECTION 3

Expressions of Faith

He will guard the feet of his faithful servants, but the wicked will be silenced in the place of darkness. (1 Samuel 2:9 NIV)

The First Christmas

His Father bid Him go
Attend a desperate woe:
Atone for human wrong,
Seek believers from the throng,
Suffer and die alone,
A ransom for God's own.
Perchance He clung unto the Father's hand.
Perhaps a moment's *Why?*
A silent, sad, *Must I?*
Then, *Abba Father, I will go—*
I understand.

Mary and Elizabeth

When miracles happen, people speculate, don't you think? This miracle of Jesus's birth, this banner of the Christian faith, certainly made me speculate—about distrust, sexism, brutality—about our charge to love the way God wants us to ... Mary and Elizabeth is a thought about two cousins discussing two miracles.

~

At that time Mary got ready and hurried to a town in the hill country of Judea where she entered Zechariah's home and greeted Elizabeth. When Elizabeth heard Mary's greeting, the baby leaped in her womb, and Elizabeth was filled with the Holy Spirit. In a loud voice she exclaimed: "Blessed are you among women, and blessed is the child you will bear! "But why am I so favored, that the mother of my Lord should come to me? As soon as the sound of your greeting reached my ears, the baby in my womb leaped for joy. Blessed is she who has believed that what the Lord has said to her will be accomplished!" (Luke 1:39–45 NIV)

Scene 1: Elizabeth welcomes Mary to her home.

Mary (*arriving a little out of breath, greets Elizabeth warmly*): Good day, blessed cousin. And greetings to you from my parents. Thank you for allowing me to come.

Elizabeth: Mary, dear, dear Mary! How nice … (*She stops speaking suddenly and raises her hands in praise to God—one hand praising, the other touching her stomach.*) Oh hallelujah! Hallelujah! (*Composing herself*) Sit down, dear.

Mary: *You* sit down, ma'am. (*Going over to Elizabeth and looking at her fearfully*) What just happened? Are you all right?

Elizabeth: Oh you precious little one! I'm quite all right! I'm just so—so— so excited. You know—you know … Or do you? Do you know that I've been told of what God has revealed to you? What do you know of this, my child?

Mary: What do I know? Oh, Elizabeth. I only know that God spoke to me. He sent His angel to tell me that I would give birth to our Messiah. He told me about you, also—that you would bear a son who would be special too. He told me not to be afraid. And I'm not, I'm not. I believe God. I believe God. But I can't help wondering, how come me. How come me?

Elizabeth: How come you, dear child? Why not you? Which of us knows the ways of our God?

Mary: That's true. God is so powerful. Who would dare question Him?

Elizabeth (*smiling*): You would, that's who. What do you think you just did?

Mary (*looking down shyly*): Oh, my Lord, forgive me. (*Then looking squarely at Elizabeth*) I am not afraid, ma'am. But I just don't understand. I just can't understand! It's too wonderful for me. But I have so many questions I dare not ask!

Elizabeth: There is no one to answer you, Mary—no one but God, and He will in His time. You've heard the sacred writings, Mary. I know your mother has taught them to you since you were old enough to hear and understand.

Mary: Yes, yes, she did, of course. And I remember all the times she spoke to me about the coming of the Messiah. Such a glorious promise!

Elizabeth: And do you remember her telling you that the Messiah would be born to a virgin?

Mary: Yes, I do remember that. And I am, of course. But there must be someone more worthy than I. You know how our family lives. Why—why—we don't even have money to buy barley sometimes. (*Blushes at the thought of telling family business.*)

Elizabeth: Mary, Zechariah and I are your family. We know your circumstances, and yes, you know ours ... I hope you don't think me insensitive to say this. But we live humbly before God just as you do. God expects all of us to live humbly before Him, whether we have wealth and station or not.

Mary: I know, I know. Mother has told me. And dear cousin, although I don't fully understand, I do know that God is with me. I know I am His handmaiden. And you know what—this is so strange. When God came to me, I had just finished my monthly mikveh. Isn't that—isn't that—well, isn't that something!

Elizabeth (*smiling*): It is—you're right; it certainly is something! Well, my dear, I don't know. But (*as a dreamy look comes upon her*) it would not surprise me that the seed would be planted when your body was fully cleansed! I do not know that for sure, of course. I'm only speculating—as all of us do when we don't really know what we're talking about! (*Both laugh.*)

Mary (*changing the mood to solemnity*): But I do know one thing for certain, Cousin Elizabeth.

Elizabeth (*smiling as one might at a delightful child*): What one thing do you know for certain?

Mary: I know for certain that I do not know what it's going to be like when I … when …

Elizabeth: When you what? When you what?

Mary: When I—I mean—when the baby begins to make Himself known on my body! What will I do? People will—people will not honor me! And my betrothed, my Joseph—what will they think of him? And what will he think of me? Surely he knows I would not betray him, but—will he honor me? He may even …

Elizabeth: Be still, my child, be still! *God* has honored you! And that's the most important thing!

Mary (*almost to herself*): God has honored me. God has honored *me*!

Scene 2 (*The next morning in Elizabeth's home. Mary and Elizabeth are seated.*)

Mary: Oh, I had such a good rest, Cousin Elizabeth. I didn't realize how tired I was!

Elizabeth: It's a distance from your home to up here in the hill country. It has been such a long time since I took the journey, but I remember it as wearying even on the donkey. You walked. How long did it take you?

Mary: About three times of sun risings and settings—but I was so eager to see you, to talk with you, that it didn't seem that long. How was it for you?

Elizabeth (*puzzled as the question doesn't make sense to her*): How was what for me?

Mary: Your baby. I mean, when you knew. Did God speak to you?

Elizabeth: No. Not so I could hear His voice. And no angel came to me. But of course I know it's God's doing. Every barren woman longs for a child, and I'm no exception. But you know I'm too old to have a baby, so what else could it be? What else?

Mary (*reaching over to hug Elizabeth*): Oh yes, yes! With God, nothing is impossible! Praise be to His name!

Elizabeth: Do you remember last night when you came? I told you that the baby leaped in my womb. I believe that even the baby knows about you and our wondrous Savior who is to come through your womb.

Mary: The sacred writings say the birth will come through our ancestor David.

Elizabeth: Yes.

Mary: And through *my* womb! Our blessed Savior! It is too wonderful! Through my womb! (*blushing*) I could almost feel your baby leap too, dear Cousin! You were so ecstatic! Bearing a child has to be the most marvelous thing in the world!

Elizabeth: It has to be!

Mary: I've heard all my life how grand you and Cousin Zechariah are. You are wealthy and yet you are so humble, always giving,

giving, giving! That you would bid me come stay with you for a time is, well, is …

Elizabeth: Hush, my child. We are both God's chosen. It is only right that we should have this time together.

Mary (*Nervously fidgeting. Both Mary and Elizabeth are quiet for a moment as if meditating on this entire conversation, when Mary speaks.*): Mother told me that Cousin Zechariah has been unable to speak since you have been with child.

Elizabeth: I don't really know what happened to Zechariah because he cannot tell me, but I know that God spoke to him. (*Excitedly*) Maybe the same angel that spoke to you spoke to Zechariah!

Mary: How does he feel? Is he angry? Is he sad?

Elizabeth: He is neither sad nor angry, neither sad nor angry. In fact he smiles all the time. He is going to become a father, and that makes him very happy.

Mary: Where is he now?

Elizabeth: Wherever God has called him in the performance of his priestly duties. He will be home soon. He'll be so glad to see you.

Mary: And I him! Oh, Cousin Elizabeth, I am so happy, so very happy to be here!

Scene 3 (*three months later still in Elizabeth' home*)

Mary (*Now the baby bump shows even in her loose clothing, and she caresses it): Isn't this precious? I have taken a new shape. (She puts her hands forward in an exaggeration of her fullness.*) I don't feel any leaping around as you did, but once in a while—once in a while, it seems as if the baby is already talking to me!

Elizabeth (*smiling*): What is He saying?

Mary: Oh, I wish I could tell you. I don't hear words exactly—just a feeling. I think He's telling me He will have many enemies one day.

Elizabeth: As all of us will who try to do God's will.

Mary: No, it's—well, I don't know, but if He's going to have enemies, I hope He doesn't have them while He's still a child. Children should not have enemies!

Elizabeth: He'll be a happy child, dear. You and Joseph will see to that. And just you wait. He'll have brothers and sisters to play with—and friends, too.

Mary: I wonder if he'll know that He's the Messiah.

Elizabeth: I think He will know. But other people will not. Not until God brings Him to that point of His life when everyone must know. You'll see. You'll see …

Mary: Isn't it wonderful to know that you'll have a child to cherish and love and teach things to and …

Elizabeth: Yes, but just remember, Mary. Yours is God's Son. And He will live under God's direction, we can be sure of that! His behavior may even seem strange to you sometimes. None of us knows the will of God for another's life. You must always remember that!

Mary (*changing the subject and playing curiously with a bit of thread on her dress*): Elizabeth, may I brush your hair now instead of waiting for your servant to come? I want to serve you. I wish I could stay longer!

Elizabeth: Your beautiful spirit will be with me long after you leave—and wherever God calls you to go. But my time is almost here. And you must return to Joseph and your parents. They will want you nearby well before *your* time comes so that they can help you prepare for …

Mary: Help me prepare for …

Elizabeth: You know, dear. Help you prepare for—help you withstand the talk, the jeers, the questions, the looks, and well … you are so young, but you'll be fine! Blessed are you among women. And blessed is the fruit of your womb, God's Son, Jesus! This child will change our lives forever—and not only ours, but those of all who will come after us. Hallelujah!

Mary: Amen!

Choir: "Blessed Assurance" (*with refrain sung only once*)

Blessed assurance, Jesus is mine!
Oh, what a foretaste of glory divine!
Heir of salvation, purchase of God,
Born of His Spirit, washed in His blood.

Perfect submission, perfect delight,
Visions of rapture now burst on my sight;
Angels descending, bring from above
Echoes of mercy, whispers of love.

Perfect submission, all is at rest,
I in my Savior am happy and blest;
Watching and waiting, looking above,
Filled with His goodness, lost in His love.

Refrain:

This is my story, this is my song,
Praising my Savior all the day long;
This is my story, this is my song,
Praising my Savior all the day long.

Hymn: "Blessed Assurance"
Public Domain

From Day To Day

Lord, let me live for Thee.
Let my life a tribute be
To the good I see in others—
My friends, my fellows, my brothers.
Keep my feet from the well-trodden path
Where people go astray
And succumb to temptation on the way.
Lord, let me live for Thee;
I know that You died for me!

The Preacher

A slight man, short even—
Only the top of his robed chest shows
Behind the podium.
He speaks a welcome;
Then, stretching his arms
Across the width of the sacred desk,
He clutches its sides and begins to rise—
Spreading the wings of his garment.
One hand pushes forward,
The other summons heaven
As he courts the souls before him,
Telling them of hope, assurance, and urgency—
Always urgency!
No longer is he slight, short even.

Think on These Thing

I talked to God today
While riding down a country road.
I asked Him, please, to help me bear
What seemed a heavy load.
When suddenly I was aware of many, many things—
The stately trees, the soft morn's breeze,
The flutter of birds' wings;
The sandy clay upon the hill,
The rustle of the grass,
The lake that breathed and yet was still—
These things had come to pass!
And then again I closed my eyes
And offered God my prayer—
Of thanks this time
For I realized
My answer was right here.
Yes, I talked to God today
Of things I couldn't see,
And on that sandy, dusty road,
The Lord talked back to me!

A Prayer for Patience
(two days before major eye surgery)

Dear God,
I was told the doctor would call in ten minutes;
It's been almost two hours!

Too many people, God!
(A famous playwright once wrote those words—
I'll borrow the words.)
"Too many people, God"—
The doctor has to attend
To too many people;
She can't attend to me right now.
I am one of the too many people!

But Lord, there are other things I want to do today
You know what I had planned—
And You know it was not a selfish plan—
Why won't she call me?
It won't take long—just two minutes of her time.
Is there nothing I can do but wait?

Well, no, but while you wait you can think on these things:
Your dear friend is facing separation from life.
Your husband just lost his job.
Your doctor has worked fourteen hours straight.
Your family loves you.
You are not blind, nor are you deaf—
The telephone is ringing. Answer it!

Thank You, Lord!

On Living

Hurrying through the park one day,
I saw a hobo gazing at the sky.
He looked for all the world as though
His life had passed him by.
Thinking of course (as most of us would)
That here was a pitiful sight,
I decided to go to offer him
Relief from his sad plight.

I sat on the bench beside him;
He heeded not my gaze,
But just kept looking toward the sky—
Almost in a daze.

Then suddenly he turned to me
(The wisest look I've ever seen)
And said, "You know, lady,
Your face looks sorta keen;
I know just what you're thinking 'bout—
That here's a sad ol' man,
A body that the world's passed by,
You'll help me if you can.

Well, lady, let me tell you,
I appreciate the thought,
But as for helping me,
Well, really I guess not.

You see, fate's been kinda good to me,
Kinder than most folks know.
It's true, I don't have a family,
And only a little dough;
But I sure am happy, lady
And I've got a right to be—
'Cause the things most folks are looking for
Are here, and they're mine for free!

Folks work all day and sleep all night,
Night dreaming and daydreaming too
Of the things that someday they will have
As soon as a raise comes through!

They plan, and save, and worry, and fret,
And life's really passing them by,
'Cause mostly they're living for what they get
And after they get it, they die!
But me, I'm just taking it easy—
I sit here all day long
And listen to the breeze whistling through the trees.
And lady, it's a beautiful song!

I think about a lot of things
You'd say don't amount to much—
But I'm happy, lady, 'cause you see,
God and me are in touch!"

~

Some years after writing this poem, I came across a newspaper story of a homeless man sitting on a bench, speaking and obviously fellowshipping with people who passed his way. Oh, was I excited—the man written about in the newspaper was a prestigious man. My hobo, at least in my opinion, was a prestigious man. Immediately I wrote a letter to the newspaper. "That's my hobo," I wrote. "You found my hobo!" With my letter, I sent a copy of my poem to the newspaper staff hoping they'd reply. They didn't!

SECTION 4

Expressions of Introspection

Ask and it will be given to you; seek and you will find; knock and the door will be opened to you. For everyone who asks receives; the one who seeks finds; and to the one who knocks the door will be opened. (Matthew 7:7–11 NIV)

Regeneration

It was just before four in the afternoon.
Quitting time couldn't come too soon.
My restless spirit had settled in gloom.

I decided to take a walk about
To conquer the doldrums—
I wanted to shout
Too much!
And no more work would I put out!

From my cramped, stuffy office I emerged,
And turning a corner, my spirit surged.
I looked across at the windowed wall—
A lovelier sight I could not recall!

The setting sun its shadows unfurled;
God had turned on the lamps of the world!
Back to my desk I went in a hurry
To finish the day in a thankful flurry—
Thankful for work and for God's intervention,
Thankful for peace in the midst of my tension!

Discovery

"Have courage," she said
"Go down and find the woman.
And when you find her, bring her here.
I *want* to know her.
You *need* to know her."
And I did.

And the going made me glad—
There are things that I like
About the woman I found.
And the going made me sad—
There are things I don't like
About the woman I found.
There are things that are lost
To the woman I found.

But finding the woman
And taking her hand
Was good!

Woman Black

Her ebony face was carved by grace,
Her body made strong by daring;
She walks, head high, with chin upraised
Through life's uncertain clearing.
She wears a look that's proud and wise,
But soft and reverent too.
She's woman—black,
And faith in God has taught her what to do!

Coming Together

There's this TV show on Sundays.
It's called *Coming Together,*
And mostly I like it.

It's about us black folk making it—
And we surely need to know about that!
Other folk do too.
But sometimes I wonder
About us coming together
I mean, I really do!

When we come together—us
Not on Sunday TV
But on every, every day—
We talk about us—and them.
Bitter talk, get even with 'em talk,
Git 'em back talk!

It's *none of them's okay*
And *some of us ain't either!*
And then it's *heavy* down
'Cause we can't see no changes
And we get mad at us,
Even more than we're mad at them!

What would it be like, I wonder
If we talked about something besides them and us
When we come together—hmm?

A Whole Lot Has Gone On!

This play was written in tribute to Mary McLeod Bethune, a pioneer in the twentieth century who challenged the inequities in America and was rightfully honored for it. This was the first play I ever wrote—again to share black history with the community in a "fun" way. Mary McLeod Bethune is deceased, but the school exists grandly as Bethune Cookman University in Daytona Beach, Florida. I was not privileged to meet Mrs. Bethune in person, but I did meet the woman in the play (not her real name) who told me her age and gave me the newspaper. Ladies and gentlemen, join me in fantasy about the life of a remarkable woman.

~

Characters

Kilsie Joseph, girl, age twelve

Shirley Borden, girl, age thirteen

Mary McLeod, bookshelf, age ten

William McLeod, bookshelf, Mary's brother

Grandmother Sophia, bookshelf, Mary's grandmother

Samuel McLeod, bookshelf, Mary's father

Sister McLeod, bookshelf, Mary's older sister

Farinda Joseph, college freshman, sister of Kilsie

Dora Little, college freshman

Celia Patterson, college freshman

Beatrice Joseph, age sixteen, sister of Kilsie

Miss Freeman, professor at Bethune Cookman College

Act 1: Yearnings

Scene: Kilsie Joseph and Shirley Borden are dressed in jeans and baseball caps, lolling on Kilsie's bed talking to each other as scene opens—music quietly playing on tape recorder

Kilsie *(rising to a sitting position):* You know what, Shirley? Christmas vacation's almost over, and our family hasn't gone anywhere special yet!

Shirley: Mine neither.

Kilsie: But Mom's taking me and Farinda and Beatrice to the museum on Sunday. She says there's a concert there she thinks we'll like. It's about spirituals. Want me to ask her if you can come?

Shirley *(sitting up):* No, thanks. Even if I don't go nowhere, I don't want to go to no concert of spirituals!

Kilsie: Why not? A concert is a lot of singing, and you like singing!

Shirley: Sure I do. But not spirituals—that old dead stuff! I like the songs I hear on my dad's tapes. Songs like the guitar players sing and dance to. You know, like *(Starts to sing a popular jazz song)*. If I do, mmm. If I do, mmm.

Kilsie: I like that too, but I'd like to learn something different, too. I don't think I've ever heard spirituals.

Shirley: No? Well, I have. I have! Mom sings them all the time. Old dead songs like this. *(Gets up from bed, sits in chair, and sings)* Nobody knows the trouble I see, nobody knows my sorrow—and sometimes she sings one that she rocks to. It goes like this—I'm a rollin', I'm a rollin', I'm a rollin' through an unfriendly world. Why she likes them, I don't know.

Kilsie: Do you think she could teach me a few?

Shirley: She'd love that. I'll ask her for you.

Kilsie: Well, for now, let's play a tape

Shirley: Okay (*putting on the tape*)

Child Mary McLeod (*smiling as she jumps onto stage*)

Shirley (*jumping up*): Hey, what's going on here? Who are you? And your clothes? You comin' or goin' to a costume party or something? Wha-a-t!

Mary: Don't be scared. My name's Mary. Say you're dreaming if you want to, but I'm here—just jumped down from your parents' bookshelf in the hall. I'm here talkin' to you from the past. Your an-ces-tral (*stressing the word*) past.

Kilsie (*goes to chair, sits down, wipes her head with disbelief*): Our what kind of past?

Mary: An-ces-tral—that means the people in your family who lived before you—your ancestors—old people, you know what I mean. Our preacher told us that one time when we was worshiping the Lord. I remembers everything our preacher says!

Kilsie: I think I know what you mean, but you're not in my family. So what do you know about our past? You're just a girl like us. How old are you, anyway?

Mary: Ten. I was born July 10, 1875.

Shirley. Oh, come on, I'm thirteen, three years older than you, and I was born in 1988. If you were born in 1875, you'd be over one hundred years old now. What do you think you're doing? Trying to pull some ghost stuff on us?

Mary: No, I'm not a ghost. I'm from an old book on your parents' bookshelf in the hall, and on the pages I come from right now, I'm ten years old! Mary McLeod, ten years old. Live in Maysville, South Carolina.

Shirley: Well, what do you want to tell us, ten-year-old Mary McLeod from Maysville, South Carolina?

Mary: I heard you all talkin' 'bout spirituals. You called them old dead music, and they ain't—I mean (*correcting herself*) they are not.

Shirley: They sound dead to me.

Mary: Well, they ain't. I mean … they are not … they alive 'cause they keeps us alive. When we' working in the fields so hard, singing 'em reminds us to keep on going, that there's a better day coming for us colored people.

Kilsie: Colored people?

Mary: That's what we're called. What's wrong with that? Just means that we got color on our skin and white folks ain't.

Shirley: Well, we're not called colored people now. What's that mean anyway? Colored purple? Red? Green? What? We're African Americans because our ancestors come from Africa and we were born in America.

Mary (*laughing and shaking her head*): Well, what do you know 'bout that? You asked me what I know about your past, and just like that you tell me that you-alls an-ces- tors (*enunciating syllables*) was African. Mine, too, don't you see. We is—I mean—we *are* family!

Shirley: I guess maybe you do know something about us, then. But about those spirituals—I heard they were slave songs. And I wouldn't let nobody make me a slave, and so I don't want to hear 'em. Is that what you are—a slave?

Mary: No, I's not a slave. Never was. Grandmother Sophia—we call her Big Mama—and Mama and Papa used to be, but they got free!

Kilsie: When?

Mary: When President Lincoln's E-man-ci-pa-tion Proc-la-ma-tion (*enunciating boldly and proudly*) came out. Mama taught me how to say those words. She can't read, but Mama's real smart. One of her African an-ces-tors was a royal prince.

Shirley: Really! That's neat ... and, yeah, I do remember reading about the Emancipation Proclamation in school!

Kilsie: Me, too! President Lincoln said that the nation could not survive half slave and half free.

Mary: And he was right. Slavery was the wrongest thing this country ever did.

Shirley (*correcting Mary's English*): The worst thing!

Mary: That's what I said. Now come on, let's go back (*waving her hands to them as if beckoning*) to the spirituals. You know that song you were listening to?

Kilsie: Yeah—

Mary: Yes, play a little of it again ... What's that thing you got there, anyway?

Kilsie: It's a tape recorder. You don't know about tape recorders? (*She picks up a tape.*) The songs are on here. We got CDs too.

Mary: There's a whole lot you could tell me, ain't there? But play the thing, please. *(Kilsie puts the tape on; they listen for a little while, then Mary speaks again.)* See that part where the leader talks and the choir sings whatever he says? *(She mimics the call-response of the tape.)*

Shirley and Kilsie: Yeah. That's what we like most about it.

Mary: Well, when we sing the work songs—you call 'em spirituals, we call 'em work songs—sometimes we do the same thing. I'll show you. *(She points to herself as she says.)* I'll be the leader like the man on your song. You be the people who sing what he tells them to sing. Ready?

Kilsie: Ready.

Mary: Every time I sing "this little light of mine," you sing, "I'm gonna let it shine." Okay?

Shirley and Kilsie: Okay.

Mary *(singing):* This little light of mine.

Shirley and Kilsie: I'm gonna let it shine.

Mary: This little light of mine.

Shirley and Kilsie: I'm gonna let it shine.

Mary: This little light of mine.

Shirley and Kilsie: I'm gonna let it shine.

Mary: Now all together, "Let it shine, let it shine, let it shine." Now let's clap to it. *(They sing together, clapping; Mary continues.)* Now wasn't that something like your singer was doing?

Kilsie: Something like it. Hey, Shirley, maybe the guy on the tape's style of singing came from the spiritual style.

Mary: I'll bet it did! Now that you've got the work song, let's sing it again!

(The girls nod and hum together, patting feet and swaying, as they sing the song through again.) This little light of mine ...

Mary: Now, you're gettin' into it. Like I told you, those kinds of songs keeps us alive while we's working and we works hard, I mean, hard, in the fields.

Kilsie: What are you doing in the fields?

Mary: Picking cotton, mostly.

Shirley: After school?

Mary: I wish. There ain't no school for colored children. We all got to work in the fields. But we's lucky. Least mama and papa get to keep the money they sell the cotton for, 'cause papa owns his own land. He ain't a sharecropper!

Kilsie: Sharecropper?

Mary: Yes, most families is sharecroppers. They works the land, but they don't own it. They only gets to keep a little bit of what the cotton sells for.

Shirley: That's not fair! (She and Kilsie thoughtfully shake their heads.) You got brothers and sisters?

Mary (proudly): Oh, yeah, I got a bunch of 'em. There's Sallie, and William, and Big Sister, and Knee Baby, and Junior, and Brother Two and Hattie, and Little Sis, and Baby Sam, and William, and Brother One, and did I say William? And ...

Shirley: Never mind. I can never remember all those names anyhow. How many of you altogether?

Mary: Oh, I dunno. 'Bout this many. *(Holding out her hands as if counting her fingers)* I dunno nothin' much about figurin'.

Kilsie: Well, I counted more than eight. And that is a whole bunch. I got seven brothers and sisters. There's Farinda—she's in college—and Beatrice, and George, and …

Shirley *(interrupting her):* Both of you got too many brothers and sisters. Should have just one like me. *(Then to Mary)* You all live together, Mary?

Mary: Nope, never did, actually. Some on different plantations. Some of 'em married and gone. We got 'bout *(starts to count on her fingers)* We got 'bout this many *(holding out her fingers just once and shrugging)* livin' home, workin' 'round, gettin' in my way. But they's all good. And Mama and Papa and Big Mama. All good.

Kilsie: You all have fun together? We do here in my house.

Mary: We sure do. We mess with each other a lot when we's in the fields—that is, till Mama call out, "Stop that foolin' around! Be dark in a minute. You know we need to get forty more pounds picked before the day is out." *(Shirley and Kilsie laugh.)*

Mary: We even have fun when, come to think of it, ain't nothing funny. Like the time Ol' Bush died.

Kilsie: Who's Old Bush?

Mary: He was our old mule. He just plop up and died while we was out working one day. Know what? I think I'll call my brother William down to tell you 'bout it. William was always funning. Papa used to get so mad at him 'cause he wouldn't ever be serious.

(Mary calls to William to come down from the book.) Willie, Willie, come on down here! Come on, Willie!

William *(enters, jumping on stage, looking all around):* You call me, little sis? Where we at? Who these gals?

Mary: We're in the future, Willie. What you think? These girls is going to be our friends.

William: Hi, little ol' gals. What you call yourselfs?

Kilsie: I'm Kilsie Joseph.

Shirley: And I'm Shirley Borden. Hi!

William: Don't pinch me. I don't want to wake up. Little ol' gals with funny looking caps on they heads, and wearing pants like boys … Well, what you want me to do, Mary?

Mary: Want you to tell them about the time Old Bush died.

William *(laughing):* You mean when we had to plow the land by ourselfs. Warn't that somethin', Mary? That were really something!

Kilsie: Well, tell us.

William *(laughing):* That day? That day? That was some day, wasn't it? We was all following the mule, Old Bush, as he broke the land for seed. But Old Bush was actin' funny. He was going so slow like this *(starting to plod like a mule)*.

Mary: And most of that ol' field still had to be plowed too.

William: Sure did. We had a lot of plowing left to do. But Ol' Bush couldn't go no farther. His eyes got all funny, and he swayed from side to side like this, and he fell, plop on the ground. *(He falls to the ground; the others laugh.)*

Mary: Yeah, I 'spect it looks funny now, but it weren't funny then. We all had to take the place of the mule.

Kilsie: You what?

William: We had to be the mule. We *was* the mule! We picked up the mule, *(bending as if picking up the mule),* carried him over to the edge of the field, buried him, and went back to the field!

Mary: Then all us took up those two straps of the harness and put them over our own shoulders. And we pulled that plow along—one of us at the time.

Kilsie: I can't believe you did that.

Shirley: Me neither.

William: Well, believe it. Right, Mary? Nobody knows the trouble *we've* seen. *(Exits)*

Mary *(as William exits):* Nobody knows! Not nobody! *(Begins humming "Nobody Knows the Trouble I've Seen" as choir enters singing.)*

Choir: Nobody knows the trouble I seen
Nobody knows my sorrow
Nobody knows the trouble I seen
Glory, hallelujah!

Sometimes I'm up, sometimes I'm down
Oh, yes, Lord
Sometimes I'm almost to the ground
Oh, yes, Lord

"Nobody Knows the Trouble I've Seen"
Negro spiritual/Public domain

Kilsie: Mary, I can see what you mean when you say your brother William is a lot of fun. But is working all you do? Don't you do anything else?

Mary: Oh, sure. We sing a lot, and we sit around the fire listening to Big Mama tell stories from the Bible. She don't read, of course, none us do. But she done heard them stories for so many years in church, she knows 'em all. If you want me to, I'll call Big Mama down from the book and let her talk to you. *(She looks towards the exit where the bookshelf is and calls.)* Grandmother Sophia, Big Mama, come on down, please!

Grandmother Sophia *(enters from exit, pipe in hand, looking around as if lost)*: Mary, Mary. You calling me? What you want chile? Where are you?

Mary *(going over to Sophia and patting her shoulder)*: I'm right here, Big Mama. And these are my friends of the future. This is Kilsie, and this is Shirley. Say hello to Big Mama, y'all. Like this. *(Curtsying to her grandmother and motioning for the girls to do likewise)*

Kilsie and Shirley: Hi, Big Mama.

Grandmother Sophia: High? Looks like I ain't up high no more! I'm down here with you. *(The girls giggle, and Mary looks at them disdainfully.)*

Mary: You don't say hi to grownups, y'all. You say, "How do you do, ma'am?" Grownups deserves a lot of respect, 'specially real old grownups like Big Mama. They deserves respect 'cause they's done a lot for they families, and they's wise, and we loves 'em. Just say, "How do ya do, Big Mama?"

Kilsie and Shirley *(giggling)*: How do ya do, Big Mama?

Grandmother Sophia: Tolerable, thank ya, young'uns! Just tolerable. The rheumatiz done got me a little, but I'm right pleased to meet you, although the good Lord knows I don't know what I'm doing here.

Mary: I called you down, Big Mama, 'cause I wanted Kilsie and Shirley to hear you tell a story from the Bible.

Big Mama: Well, chile, I'd be right pleased to do that. Which one ya want me to tell 'em?

Mary: You know the one, Big Mama? About the people who was free after lots of years in slavery. The story of Queen Esther pleading with the king for her people.

Grandmother Sophia (*dramatically chanting*): Well, for seventy years God's people were in Babylon.

Mary: Yes, yes!

Grandmother Sophia: Seventy years bowed down under the rule of crazy kings in crazy lands.

Mary: Oh, mah Lord!

Grandmother Sophia: Then a new king Cyrus came to rule—he better than the other kings!

Mary: And prophet Jeremiah rubbed his eyes and raised his head, Lord, Lord!

Grandmother Sophia: And then this Cyrus showed that he was not cruel like the kings who went before him!

Mary: And a prophet clapped his hands and shouted!

Grandmother Sophia; Yes he did, yes he did—he said, "Comfort ye, comfort ye my people. Tell Jerusalem that huh exile is over. Her sins is forgiven! Make straight in the desert a highway for our God. We's—free at—last."

Mary: Hallelujah!

Grandmother Sophia: And amen and amen!

Kilsie and Shirley *(clapping and swaying)*: Hallelujah, free. Hallelujah, free. Hallelujah, free. Hallelujah, free! We's free at last!

(Off stage choir sings)

Woke up this morning with my mind
Stayed on Jesus!
Woke up this morning with my mind
Stayed on Jesus!
Woke up this morning with my mind
Stayed on Jesus!
Hallelu, hallelu, Hallelujah!

"Woke up this Morning with My Mind Stayed on Jesus"
Negro spiritual, Public Domain

Kilsie and Shirley *(clapping)*: Big Mama, listen, the angels are singing for you!

Mary *(laughing)*: Sure they are, gals. They're singing a spiritual. We sing it at home a lot, don't we, Big Mama?

Grandmother Sophia: Sure do! *(Starts humming)*

Mary *(interrupting)*: But you know what I think about lots, Big Mama?

Grandmother Sophia: What, chile?

Mary: We's free, and it's good that we don't belong nobody but ourselfs, but in another way we ain't free.

Grandmother Sophia: In what way, Mary?

Mary: Well, we ain't got nice things like the white folks got. Massah Wilson's house is bee-yoo-ti-ful! Ours nice, but not like that, and …

Grandmother Sophia: Don' call him Massah Wilson, Mary. He ain't our massah no more. Just call him *Mister* Wilson. And don't fret yourself with what you ain't got. Just praise the good Lord for all you do got. A family what loves you a heap—and your good health!

Mary: I know, I know, Big Mama! We got a lot to be thankful for! But I cain't help thinkin' we'd have more if we could read.

Shirley: I don't even like readin'. I don't think it's all that important. Why do you think it's so important, Mary?

Mary: Well, Shirley, when I was over Massah—I mean *Mister* Wilson's—house t'other day gettin' washin' for mama to do, I seed lots of books around, and John—he's only ten years old like me—he can read all of 'em. And I just think that's how come they got so much. Everybody kin read and get a job and everything!

Grandmother Sophia: Mary, you know y'all got no time for learnin' to read. Even if there was a way. And there ain't!

Mary: I knows, Big Mama—I mean—I know! But I just want to read so bad I kin taste it. (*Emphasizing*) A whole lot's going on in this world, and I want to be a part of it. And I'm gonna, Big Mama. I'm gonna!

Kilsie (*to Shirley as Mary and Big Mama exit*): I'll bet she will, Shirley … and you know, I'm going to put my mind to working harder in school—like my sister Farinda does.

Shirley: Me too. Maybe reading will be fun then. I just might read that book Mary jumped out of!

Kilsie: Me too. *(Puts head back dreamily)* Well, that sure is a way for us to go back in history and see it for ourselves. Somehow I think that Mary McLeod did a lot for us as black people.

Shirley; Yeah, maybe …

Act 2—Strivings
Scene 1: The McLeod Homestead

Samuel: Hello, all you folks out there. Guess you're wonderin' where you are. Well, you're at the McLeod Homestead; you're on my farm. You kin call it dreamin' if you want, or maybe some li'l ol gal named Kilsie got you here, but somehow, y'all have just stepped back into history—1896 to be exact. How ya be? Mighty proud to have this chance to talk to ya!

My Mary tell me she walked into the future when she about ten years old, talkin' to couple of gals name Kilsie and Shirley, tellin' 'em about us. Shore was happy when she come back to the book. Asked me if there was any way I could get a small crowd to come up to the book. Ah couldn't think of a way, but my wife Patsy—she'll be along pretty soon—she figured out a way, and here I am.

Name's Samuel—just plain *Samuel* used to be. Now it's Samuel McLeod. Ya see, I was born and come up on the McLeod plantation in Maysville, North Carolina. Used to be a slave—don't you know.

Well, Old Massah McLeod warn't a bad sort, and he didn't give us a real bad time. After the E-man-si-pa-shun Prok-la-ma -shun, he give me his other name—the name I'll go through with for the rest of my life—McLeod. Yes suh! Samuel McLeod! Samuel McLeod!

Got married to the sweetest little ol' gal; her name Patsy. She belonged to the McIntosh farm, and Massah McLeod and Massah McIntosh let me and my Patsy get married. Yes, we did, we got us married—jumped over the broom and all, just as sure as you please. Had us quite a little weddin'! Then we got to havin' chillun. Had seventeen young'uns in all, some of 'em taken away to other plantations.

Guess we'd a gone on workin' for Massah McLeod till ol' man death come to claim us, but the Civil War come along and we got freed when it was over! Oh, wasn't that a mighty day, a mighty day! Folks runnin' and singin', runnin' and laughin', runnin' and cryin', but runnin', runnin', runnin'!

Guv'mint promised all o' us forty acres and a mule, but a lot of us didn't get that! Well, I done tol' you I was married to the sweetest little ol' gal this side of the Mississippi. Patsy kept on workin' for ol' Massah McIntosh and earned enough to buy the first five acres of this place we's standin' on—you and me. We calls it "The Homestead." Our chillun and us worked it. Then as our boys got big and went to work on other farms, they done saved enough to buy another thirty acres. We got thirty-five acres of land—almost forty—right here!

And I don't mind tellin' ya, I'm a mighty proud man. Mighty proud! It's hard work keepin' it goin', but it's ours. Keep every penny we earn. Yessuh!

It's a funny thing about cotton. It grows so slow, you'd think you wouldn't get tired pickin' it, but you do all the same!

See that ol' grapevine over there? (*Pointing to imaginary grapevine*) Well, jes' over there is where we has our Independence Day celebration. Yes, we celebrate Independence Day even though we wasn't independent when it came on July 4, 1776. We don't celebrate it so much 'cause the United States was born on that day—though we's glad of that. We celebrates it because two of our young'uns—Mary and Hattie—was born in July, and they born after we was free.

Oh, I wish y'all could come to one of them celebrations. All the food you can eat for a year and all the fun you can have for all your life!

Can I tell you something about my little Mary? Don't like folks to think I'm particular about any one of my children. The good Lord knows I love 'em all. But that Mary, she different. Dreamy sort of. Always thinkin' about God, about us and white folk, 'bout everything. Mary different, that's all. She about twenty years old now. She ain't here. She up in Chi-cah-go!

You know what she said to me one day when she was just a little thing? She went to the Wilson house to pick up some washin' for her mama and she come back home all sad. I asked her what was the matter, but all she'd say was, "What, what, Papa? What? Why we so poor and white folks so rich? Is it because they kin read and we can't."

I just shook my head. "Mary, I don't know," I said.

And she said, "I do know, Papa. It's 'cause of readin', and I'm goin' to learn to read. Write, too! I'm gonna, Papa, I'm gonna!"

She wanted to read so bad. She went around pretendin' she was readin' stuff offa anythin' she saw letters on. So I prayed, and I prayed, and we all prayed, 'specially Mary, and finally God sent us somebody.

I found out later that this lady didn't have much eddication herself, but she had a whole heap more than all us had. She'd been up north and got sent down to Maysville to start a school for colored chillun in Maysville.

We really couldn't spare any of our chillun to go to school—we had so much work tryin' to make ends meet. But we had a family meetin', and all us agreed that Mary should go. And wasn't that a mighty day? A mighty, mighty day!

Mary was out in the field when I told her. She walked from shrub to shrub of cotton plants singin' her heart out. *(Pantomimes walking around picking cotton. Chants what Mary was singing— I'm gonna read. I'm gonna read. I'm gonna get edjicated.)*

And this old heart of mine was singing too, don't ya know, 'cause I was praisin' the Lord! *(Sings)* "Oh, Lord, I thank ya, thank ya, thank ya; Lord, I thank ya, thank ya, I jes' thank ya all the days of my life!" *(He repeats the song, waving hands and swaying as he sings)* And Mary was her teacher's prize pupil. Yes, indeed. I can hear that lady now in that sweet little high bird voice of hers. *(Mocks the teacher) Mr. Sam*—she always call me Mr. Sam—"Mr. Sam, your little Mary's goin' far. She is, I know it. The other children don't come to school every day. But Mary, Mary, oh, your Mary—I know sometimes she's tired. I can see it. But she never stops, and does all her homework! She's a soldier all right enough, Mr. Sam!" *(Choir enters singing "Do You Think I'll Make a Soldier," and Samuel remains in fixed position until choir exits.)*

Do you think I'll make a soldier?
Do you think I'll make a soldier?
Do you think I'll make a soldier?
Soldiers of the cross?

We are climbing Jacob's ladder,
We are climbing Jacob's ladder,
We are climbin' Jacob's ladder,
Soldiers of the cross!

Every round goes higher and higher,
Every round goes higher and higher,
Every round goes higher and higher,
Soldiers of the cross!

Sinner, do you love my Jesus?
Sinner do you love my Jesus?
Sinner, do you love my Jesus?
Soldiers of the cross!

If you love Him, why not serve Him?
If you love Him, why not serve Him?
If you love Him, why not serve Him?
Soldiers of the cross!

Negro Spiritual
"Do You Think I'll Make a Soldier?"
Public Domain

Samuel: Well, folks, I'm a mite tired now. Rough day. Real rough. Look at these hands. *(Holds out his hands to audience)* Feel like they going to fall off at the wrist. I ain't complainin', though. God is good! But I'll just go rest a spell, so I kin keep on rollin' through this unfriendly world! *(Leaves the stage)*

Scene 2 (*same as Scene 1*)

Samuel (*entering*): Well, howdy again, y'all. Did you rest up a bit? Well, there's a whole lot more to tell you about my Mary. She did more than inch along. That girl did jes' 'bout everything!

While Miss Wilson was teachin' her readin' and writin' and figurin', she was coming home teaching it to her brothers and sisters after supper.

Then after Miss Wilson done taught her everything she knowed, Mary got the chanct to go to a couple more schools—Bible school included—Moody something.

And God fearin'! Mary loves God more than anyone I know—anyone cept'n maybe my Patsy! She jes' wanted to do the Lord's work! Started doin' it while she was still in school. Become a missionary right there in Chi-cah-go!

And ya know, the Lord's work ain't easy—no, suh! Well, y'all know that anyhow, don't ya? Mary wrote us all a letter telling us 'bout something awful but wonderful that happened when she was a missionary. Here, I'm gonna call Sister to read the letter Mary wrote about it. She's the one can read the best—after Mary, of course!

Sister (*from off stage*): I hears Papa calling me? Where ya be, Papa?

Samuel: I'm right here, Sister. Come on out here. I needs ya to read something for me.

Sister (*entering stage, wearing dress over her clothes as a liturgical dancer, looking to the left and right, and out into the audience, blinking her eyes*): Who's all these folks?

Samuel: They've joined us in history just a little ways, Sister, and I been talking to 'em about lots of things—including Mary and what all she's been doing. Want you to read that letter we got from her about that missionary business! Got it right here in my pocket. *(Takes it out and hands it to Sister.)*

Sister: Well, I'll try, Papa. You know I don't read all that good, but I'll try. *(She takes letter from Samuel and starts to read it.)* Dear Mama …

Samuel: No, don't start there. Start with the address. I want these folks to know for sure that she in Chi-cah-go.

Sister *(starts letter over at address)*: 76 LaSalle Street, Chi-cah-go. *(Throwing up her hands)* Oh, I can't read all these words! They'll just have to believe us that Mary's a missionary in Chi-cah-go.

Samuel: Oh, awright, Sister, thank you. Don't want to burden ya! *(To audience)* See, none o' us kin read much at-all. *(To Sister)* You can go on back to whatsomever you was doing, Sister, if you want, or stay here with us if you want …

Sister: I'll go back, Papa. I was doin' some washin'—need to get back to it. *(She leaves stage.)*

Samuel: Well, folks, I sure thanks ya for visitin' with me. When y'all gets back into the future, I knows you'll find some books about my Mary, 'cause I knows she gonna do great things! Been doin' things ever since she born. And now, she sho' nuff leanin' on Jesus, and He goin'to take her far. You'll just see. *(Gives a wave to the audience)* T'was real nice jawin' with ya. God bless ya!

Act 3—Legacy
Scene 1: Living room of the Joseph family, Christmas vacation. Farinda, Kilsie's older sister, has begun study at Bethune-Cookman College, and she and Kilsie are listening to music on the tape recorder.

Farinda, pacing, keeps looking at her watch. Her classmates Celia and Dora enter. Dora has a laminated newspaper behind her back.

Farinda (*walks toward them, pats one on shoulder, saying*): Hi, I was wondering if something happened. You all were supposed to be here at three o'clock. It's almost four! (*Dora and Celia look sheepish as they shrug their shoulders.*)

Farinda (*goes to tape recorder and turns it off, indicating that Kilsie should leave*): Bye, Kilsie!

Kilsie: Aw! (*Running off stage right*)

Farinda (*motions for Dora and Celia to sit. Celia does not sit, instead looks all around the room as if admiring it. Then she stops at the table with the books on it. Dora sits.*)

Dora: Sorry we're late. Time just slipped away. I got talking to Mrs. Brown. (*Puts newspaper on floor*) She's a friend of my grandmother in St. Louis, but she lives here. When I told my grandmother I was going to Bethune-Cookman College, she wanted me to go see Mrs. Brown.

Farinda: Why?

Dora: Because Mrs. Brown is ninety-two years old and actually met Mrs. Bethune.

Farinda: Ninety-two years old! I can't believe it! My goodness! Well, anyway, I'm sure glad you guys could come over. Here it is almost the end of our vacation and we're just getting together to do our reports on Mary McLeod Bethune.

Celia (*going over to sit on the sofa*): Actually it was a fun assignment. At school, they talked about Mrs. Bethune when we had orientation in the fall, so we already knew something about her. To read a whole book about her was great. I loved it!

Dora: Me, too! And Mrs. Pearl Brown really helped me today too.

Farinda: How?

Dora (*reaching for her laminated newspaper and showing it dramatically*): With this! Mrs. Brown gave me this!

Farinda: What is it?

Dora: A copy of a Daytona Beach newspaper written twenty-five years ago, the day they announced that a statue of Mrs. Bethune would be unveiled in Washington, DC.

Farinda: Oh, can I see that? (*Dora hands her the paper, and Farinda reads from it.*) At 10:30 a.m. on …

Dora: Mrs. Brown was in Daytona Beach at the time. And she went to the unveiling! She said there were thousands of people there! (*Farinda continues to read the newspaper silently.*) You all can make copies if you want.

Celia: If we want? You bet we do. We'll be the stars of the show with this when we give our reports at school next week.

Dora (*getting up, putting hands on hips*): Don't you want to know how Mrs. Brown knew Mrs. Bethune?

Celia (*walking over to table and picking up a book, thumbing through it and laughing at Dora*): I was with you when she told you, but I know you want to tell it, so go ahead.

Dora: Mrs. Brown became a youth worker with Mrs. Bethune when she started the NYA.

Farinda: What's the NYA?

Dora: The National Youth Association. It was a program to help kids who were starting down the wrong way.

Farinda: And?

Dora: Well, Mrs. Bethune introduced Mrs. Brown to her future husband. He was a youth worker with the program too. Larry Brown died last year, but he and Mrs. Brown stayed married sixty-four years!

Farinda: My goodness!

Celia: Mrs. Brown told us that the NYA was a really great organization. Saved a lot of kids from becoming hoboes, hitchhikers, and stowaways.

Farinda: Hoboes? Stowaways?

Dora *(laughing and shrugging)*: I guess we'd just call them "homeless" now. No place to stay. No job to go to. Roaming the streets, hiding in trucks so they could go somewhere else. Kids just didn't know what to do with themselves. *(Girls all nod their heads knowingly as Dora continues.)* We need something like that now, actually—same thing's happening!

Farinda: We sure do. Some of my brothers' friends have gotten into real trouble with drugs and stuff—no job—don't know what to do with themselves!

Celia *(leaning back, hand on face as if a light just came on for her):* Hey, maybe we can find out more about how to organize something like that and start it when we get out of college!

Kilsie (*entering and interrupting, standing by table*): Farinda, Mom says do you want her to fix you all some hot chocolate? She has to go out for a little while, so she wants to know *now*! (*Farinda ignores her. Kilsie raises her voice, hands on hips saying loudly.*) Farinda, I said do you want some hot chocolate? Are you deaf?

Farinda (*looking first at Kilsie, then gesturing toward the others in introduction*): Oh sorry! Celia, Dora, meet my sister Kilsie. She's twelve and feeling grown.

Kilsie (*picking up hat from the table and throwing it at Farinda*): You're the one thinks she's grown—just 'cause you're away at college, you ain't so bigetty, big Miss Amen!

Celia: Why do you call her Miss Amen?

Kilsie: 'Cause she's always saying *Amen* to everything. Haven't you heard her back at college?

Celia: Well, to tell you the truth, Kilsie, we didn't know each other very well at college. We just have one class together.

Dora: It's a long story, Kilsie. Farinda and I knew each other from Boston, and I found out that Celia would be in this area for the holidays—

Celia: So we arranged to get together because we all have to do a report on Mary McLeod Bethune for that class.

Farinda (*going to table and getting one of the Bethune books, standing there*): Don't bother telling her all that, you guys. She's just nosy anyway!

Dora (*picking up a magazine from the coffee table*): Oh, don't say that, Farinda. I wish I had a sister—and you've got four of them!

Kilsie (*laughing*): I don't pay her no mind, Dora. She ain't heavy. She's my sister. (*Goes over to Farinda and hugs her.*)

Farinda (*playfully pushing Kilsie away; all four girls laugh as Farinda walks over and sits in chair, talking as she walks*): Yes, I've got four of them—bless their little pea-picking hearts. And three brothers. My brothers are all married and living far away.

Dora: Too bad!

Celia: Sure is!

Farinda: Yeah, I miss them, but they come with their wives a couple of times a year and then we party, party, party! You should see them with my little sister Kilsie. Not supposed to have favorites, but I think she's theirs. She really is funny, I have to admit.

Celia: How?

Farinda: Oh, I don't know. She just is. She's a dreamy little kid, and something different is always happening with her. As a matter of fact, the other day she told me this wild story about Mary McLeod Bethune jumping out of that biography we have on the shelf (*gesturing toward exit*) and talking to her.

Dora (*waving her hand*): Aw, come on!

Farinda: No, true. And I told her she was just dreaming, but no, she says it really happened.

Beatrice: Aw, Farinda, she knows it was just a dream. She likes getting to you, is all.

Farinda: Then the next day, she told me that a whole lot of other people went back in history and were talking to Mrs. Bethune's father and big sister.

Celia: You're right. She's wild! Are your parents worried about her?

Farinda: Naw, my grandma says my mom used to be just like Kilsie when she was little. (*Gets up from chair, laughs and mocks her grandmother, pointing her finger and talking.*) Your mother, Farinda, had the whoppingest, wickedest imagination that God, Himself, has ever seen!" (*Everybody laughs and pretends they are falling out.*)

Beatrice (*exiting while talking*): I'm going to tell Mom you're putting out family secrets!

Farinda (*yelling after her*): Don't you dare! (*Gesturing to the others*) Come on, guys. Let's go in the kitchen and meet Mom. Then we really got to get to work and figure out these reports.

Dora and Celia: Okay. (*All exit*)

Scene 2: Classroom at Bethune Cookman College. Five or six chairs to represent classroom and an imaginary window; at left, table with tape recorder on it, chair and chalkboard; Farinda, Celia, and Dora enter, where the teacher is adjusting things on her table. Students enter with report folders in hand.

Miss Freeman: Good morning, girls. Welcome back. I hope you had a great vacation.

Celia (*taking a seat and putting her folder on the floor*): We sure did, Miss Freeman. I loved being in Boston. It was my first time there, and everybody was so nice!

Dora (*switching herself over to Miss Freeman*): And wait till you hear my news, Miss Freeman.

Miss Freeman: What?

Dora (*twirling around toward her seat and then sitting in front seat*): Can't tell you yet. It'll be in my report. (*Puts her folder on floor*)

Miss Freeman (*smiling as other girls laugh at Dora*): Oh, yes, your reports. Did you enjoy doing them?

Farinda: We really did! It was a lot of fun working together on them. We talked about our favorite parts—we even got to acting out some of them. (*Bounces around in her seat as if acting*) That made it *so* great!

Miss Freeman: What were some of your favorite parts, Farinda?

Farinda (*looking at Dora and winking, then saying to Miss Freeman*): They're in my report, Miss Freeman! In my report! (*Laughs, as does Miss Freeman*)

Miss Freeman: Well, let's get started. But before you read your actual reports, I really would like to hear about the parts of Mrs. Bethune's biography that you liked best. (*Turns and writes "Holt" on the chalkboard.*) Did all of you read the one by Rackham Holt, the best known of the biographers?

Dora: We all read that one, although I must admit I was tempted to read a shorter one. (*Miss Freeman shakes her head, and Dora giggles.*) But the librarian said the shorter one was more for children—that I'd get more out of the Holt one.

Farinda: Well, I read two, Miss Freeman. The Holt one and one by Catherine Peare (*Miss Freeman writes Peare on the chalkboard, as Farinda continues speaking.*) Hey, Miss Freeman, can I ask you something?

Miss Freeman: Not *hey, Miss Freeman*—and not *can I*, but sure. Go ahead. Ask me.

Farinda: Sorry. (*Lowering her head, then raising it and continuing*) Why are some of the facts about Mary McLeod Bethune's life different in different books?

Miss Freeman: What do you mean?

Farinda: About the mule, for example. In Catherine Peare's book, it says that the mule —Old Bush—died when Mary McLeod was a little girl working in the field with her brothers and sisters and that they buried the mule by the side of the road and went on pulling the plow themselves.

Miss Freeman: And what does it say about that in the Holt biography?

Farinda: It says that Old Bush died after Mary was grown, that she was earning money, and a new mule cost $200, and that she sent it to her family to buy a new mule.

Miss Freeman (*coming around and half sitting on table*): Farinda, that's a good point. Most biographies are what we call biographical fiction. (*Writes "biographical fiction" on the board as girls frown and look at each other quizzically*) They are based on fact, but some parts of them—especially conversations—are made up by the biographers.

Celia: Well, how can they do that? Isn't that being dishonest?

Miss Freeman (*walking back to front of table*): No, because readers expect that all things can't be recalled exactly. (*Pause.*) People who write biographies get their information from many different sources—sketchy notes written by the famous people themselves, conversations with people who actually knew them, newspaper articles, and so on. So writers have to use their common sense and imagination while being as true as they can to all the information that is available to them.

Celia *(holding her head):* I never thought of that!

Miss Freeman: Just think about your own conversations, Celia. Suppose you wanted to write down the conversations you and Dora and Farinda had when you were doing your reports. Would you be able to recall them word for word?

Celia: Probably not. And I was right there! *(All laugh.)* I see what you mean.

Miss Freeman *(sitting in chair):* Well, Celia, suppose we start our session with you. What parts of Mrs. Bethune's life story stand out for you?

Celia *(standing):* I liked how she was so smart that she made other people do the right thing. Like the time she saved her father from being cheated. Here, let me read it to you. I wrote this part into my report. *(Reaches to floor to get folder, opens folder, and fumbles to find her place.)*

Miss Freeman: She was smart! She let Mr. Eli know that she knew he was cheating her father, but she did it in a nice way. Most people couldn't have done that.

Farinda: But why should she care if she made Mr. Eli mad? He was wrong!

Miss Freeman: Because she knew that if she made Mr. Eli mad, her father would lose him as a customer altogether.

Celia: And, too, I remember reading that Mary was essentially always a missionary—trying to help people turn from wrong doing to good doing—through the teachings of Jesus.

Miss Freeman: There are so many examples of that in her story. (*Goes to chalkboard, writes "missionary" next to Mrs. Bethune's name.*)

Dora: I liked the part where she started her school and got all those important people to help her.

Miss Freeman (*writes "educator" on the chalkboard*): Yes, she did have some pretty important people to help her, and they stayed with her to the end. Educator was in her blood!

Dora: Yeah. She started with $1.50 and a city dump she had to clean up, and she got people like Mr. Gamble from a big soap-producing company and Mr. White from a big sewing machine company to donate thousands and thousands of dollars to her school!

Miss Freeman: And speaking of important people, Mrs. Bethune was advisor to five US presidents, all of whom respected her work to the heights! (*Writes "advisor to presidents" on the chalkboard.*)

Farinda: I was interested in all those organizations she started, 'cause offshoots of them are still around. She started the National Colored Women's League, for example. Now all over the country there are African American women's groups trying to do the same things she was trying to. (*Miss Freeman writes "organizer-founder" on the chalkboard.*)

Dora: Yeah. In St. Louis, there's one. My grandmother belongs to it. They have lots of things on black culture and history, and they're doing a lot for young people!

Farinda: There's a group like that in Boston, too. They helped me work out some problems when I was in high school. I didn't know Mary McLeod Bethune had anything to do with that!

Miss Freeman (*walking toward exit right, opens an imaginary window, saying as she walks*): She did—probably any black women's group in America today was influenced by the work of Dr. Bethune.

Dora: And Miss Freeman, I especially liked the part where she dealt with the Klu Klux Klan. Putting all those lights on in the school and daring the Klan to come get them. She was one brave lady!

Farinda (*nodding*): She was an all kind of lady!

Miss Freeman (*smiling*): A real Renaissance woman! (*Girls look at her quizzically as they don't understand what a Renaissance woman is.*)

Farinda: Yeah! She could do anything! The books said her singing as a missionary brought many converts to the Lord, and that she sang so well she could have been on the concert stage!

Miss Freeman: But I don't think Mrs. Bethune was all that interested in promoting herself as such. She wanted most of all just to help black people get the place in life that they deserved.

Celia (*leaning in her chair, then gesturing with her hands to make her point*): I could see that, but there was one thing I didn't like.

Miss Freeman: What was that?

Celia: Well, the book said that when Mrs. Bethune did anything, she really wanted to be sure that white people would support it. That sounds a little Uncle Tom to me.

Miss Freeman: You're not the only one who feels that way, Celia. Many people didn't like that about her—but people felt the same way about Booker T. Washington. And think about it. It was *her* technique. Look at that business with Mr. Eli.

Farinda (*looking at Celia*): Yeah, she felt she'd fail if white people didn't support her. After all, they were the majority. They had all the say.

Celia: Maybe you're right, but I still don't like it.

Miss Freeman: And Mrs. Bethune herself would have said amen to that, Celia. She wanted our people to think for themselves even if they didn't agree with her. But she knew what she had to do, and if some of her own people didn't like it, so be it. She had to be Mary McLeod Bethune!

Dora: I loved her last will and testament, and I copied it into my report. (*Points to her report on the floor, then says*) It's a wonderful legacy for us as African American young people. I'm sure going to try to live up to it. A whole lot has gone on in our country, and it's up to us to fix it.

Miss Freeman: I'm glad you said that, Dora. A whole lot has gone on in black history to help us recognize and fulfill our great potential—and Mrs. Bethune is one of our greatest heroes. As you all know after reading her biography, Mrs. Bethune did a lot more than start this college.

Girls: Mmm, she sure did.

Miss Freeman: Now, I'm ready to hear you read your full reports, but before you do, I have a surprise for you! Mrs. Bethune recorded her last will and testament and I have a copy on tape. Listen. (*Plays tape of Mrs. Bethune reading her last will and testament. All listen quietly, almost reverently, until Farinda says*)

Farinda: Amen!

Resources:

Mary McLeod Bethune: A Biography, by Rackham Holt/Doubleday, New York, 1964.

Mary McLeod Bethune, by Catherine O. Peare/Vanguard Press, NY, (c) 1951.

Great Women in the Struggle, by Igus, Patrick, Ellis, and Wesley, Just Us Books, NJ 1991.

SECTION 5

Expressions of Pain and Contemplation

I will declare your name to my people; in the assembly I will praise you. You who fear the Lord, praise Him! (Psalm 22:22–23a NIV)

One day, a young woman from our church called and asked if she could come to see me. She wanted to talk with me about writing a play for Women's Day at the church, and she had a particular scripture in mind for the theme: Ecclesiastes 4:9. With this young woman's heart directing my pen, *Super Sister Keepers* was born.

Super Sister Keepers

Characters, in order of appearance

Janet Edlin, early thirties, disturbed woman, erstwhile friend of
Mercedes Montague, early thirties, best friend of
Tanya Lothrop, early thirties.
Margaret Birdy, late forties, married, friend of Mercedes.
Mrs. Elaine Hope, mideighties, friend of Mercedes.
Kimberly Edlin, fourteen, half-sister of Janet Edlin.

Synopsis: Mercedes and Tanya return to Mercedes's home after a Saturday afternoon Bible study. As they talk about the experience, an acquaintance, Janet Edlin, comes to mind and becomes their focus. While they are talking, they receive three visitors: Margaret Birdy, who needs to rest awhile as she waits for a friend; Mrs. Elaine Hope, who stops by because she is in the neighborhood; and Kimberly, who is looking for Mercedes's brother Hubert.

As each character interacts with the other, the audience learns of their strengths and frailties; they also learn that each woman is potentially a "super sister-keeper."

The Prologue

Janet Edlin *(moaning)*: Okay, here I am, Janet Marie Edlin, the world's worst person. Never do anything right. Nobody likes me but Hubert. Not even my family cares. Those old cousins used to be around all the time. Now all they want to do is have family reunions every five years. But day-to-day caring about you, no way! They never call. Used to have friends—so-called. They only call when they need something. That's about it. So, I don't answer the telephone anymore!

You'd think somebody would come by sometime, though, wouldn't you? But even if people came by, how could I expect them to stay and visit with Ma acting the way she does. She's so mean! She's always been "funny time," but I never would have thought she'd be this mean! Always crying about the men in her life—or not in her life. So two husbands left her. So what! Men leave all the time. You gotta just take 'em as you find 'em.

(Softening a little) I'm really glad I've got my boyfriend Hubert, though. He's a sweetheart, although he does get on my nerves sometimes. Especially when he's throwing his goody-goody sister Mercedes up in my face. Says to me *(mocking the way Hubert talks)* "Sweetie, why don't you just talk to Mercedes? She only wants to be your friend." She does not. Only friend she wants is that two-faced Tanya Lothrop. Got no room for anybody else in her friend circle. So what? Who needs her? Certainly not me. And besides, who wants to hear her talk about God all the time? What's God ever done for me? Give me a sick, sick mother—I don't even know her anymore!

And that bratty Kim for a sister. Who needs a teenager for a sister? I'm thirty-three years old, for goodness sake. Kim's fourteen. I need someone I can talk to, not a kid sister who doesn't know how to spoon-feed herself. Why did Ma have to get married again, anyway? My stepfather's not the nicest guy in the world! Especially after Ma started getting sick. I was only nineteen, for goodness sake. I did the best I could, but she's still sick, sick, sick, and Kim hates me! Oh God, what have I done to deserve this? *(Goes offstage as the play begins.)*

The Play

Setting: Large kitchen, with exits stage right and stage left. Tables large enough to seat four people, four chairs, sink and door at stage right and stage left. Teacups and saucers are on the table. Mercedes and Tanya sit and sip from them.

Mercedes *(slumping in her chair and letting her hands fall by her side):* That was some discussion in Bible study today. Sure gave us something to think about.

Tanya *(elbows on table)*: Yeah. Cain and Abel. Jealousy—it's something else, isn't it? Made Cain kill his brother. But weren't you all stretching it a bit making Cain's question about being his brother's keeper our question?

Mercedes *(straightening up)*: Why? I think it was a good analogy. Cain asked the question after he had killed his brother as if to say. "How should I know where my brother is? He's not my responsibility."

Tanya: I know that. So?

Mercedes: As his brother, Cain would have been expected to know where Abel was. Families usually care for each other that way.

Tanya: That's the point. Abel was Cain's blood brother. But he killed him. His response was logical. What's he going to say, "I just killed Abel and he's lying out there in the field"? No, he had to pretend he didn't know anything about his brother's whereabouts.

Mercedes (*thinking*): Well, maybe—but the question is still relevant. Makes you aware that it's possible to be super cruel to those you're supposed to love the most.

Tanya: Granted. But the way you all were talking was as if everybody is responsible for everybody else.

Mercedes: I think you missed the point.

Tanya: Well, what was the point?

Mercedes: That we need to reach out more—to care about and try to understand what others are going through—to treat them as God would want us to treat a brother or a sister.

Tanya: You going somewhere with this? (*Waiting for an answer, but Mercedes simply looks at her thoughtfully as she continues*) Yeah … you are going somewhere with this. You're thinking about Janet Edlin, aren't you? You want to get some campaign going to butt into her business. You are always thinking about her, aren't you?

Mercedes (*smiling—she's been found out!*): Oh, you make it sound like I want to be a nosy do-gooder. That's not where I'm coming from. It's just that Janet, well, she's so different from the way she was in high school. She was always so happy-go-lucky—nice girl, didn't swear or anything like that. Now she's just the opposite. And she's just alienating all of her friends. I hate to see her like this.

Tanya: She's got your brother Hubert and sounds like she's still got you.

Mercedes: Yes, she's got my brother Hubert. But me ... she doesn't want to talk to me. Hubert doesn't talk much about her either—not to me anyway. He did tell me, though, that her mother has serious dementia and that her little sister, Kim, never wants to help with their mother. Janet says that Kim has become the brattiest teenager the world has ever known.

Tanya (*throwing her hands in the air with disdain*): I suppose now you're going to tell me that Kim and Janet are like Mary and Martha in the Bible—with Janet doing everything right and Kim doing everything wrong!

Mercedes: That's it—although I *wasn't* thinking about Mary and Martha. But what if someone or something could lead Janet to really sit at Jesus's feet as Mary did?

Tanya (*presumably not listening to what Mercedes is saying*): Everybody has problems! You, me, everybody! All Janet has to do is get her mother to a doctor and get some teen counseling for her sister. If you want to butt in, go ahead. Tell her to do that. (*Sarcastically*) Make her listen to you!

Mercedes (*pointedly*): Do you get *anything* out of going to church and Bible study?

Tanya: Oh come on now, Miss Holier than Thou. Of course, I do. But we're different, you know.

Mercedes: That's true. I'm sorry I said that.

Tanya: It's okay. It's just that when I've tried to tell people about the Lord's way of doing things, it's like throwing water on a duck's back. Not only are they not interested in what I have to say, they get downright mad that I dared to douse 'em!

Mercedes: I think I know what you mean. But if you get close enough to throw the water, don't you think that maybe just a tiny bit of it might stay on the duck's back and get absorbed into its skin?

Tanya: Not a drop.

Mercedes (*pausing, then continuing with her thoughts about Janet*): Janet is our sister—and she needs our help.

Tanya: Janet is not my sister—not my blood sister, and certainly not my sister in Christ. She doesn't even come near the church!

Mercedes: Church membership is not necessarily the answer! She's your sister *because of Christ*, and right now she needs a sister-keeper to help her with that! As my father would say, *there's a spiritual solution to every problem.* I think being a keeper means that we have to pray and listen for God's word to show us how to help others. And I think you and I need to do that together on Janet's behalf. Think we can?

Tanya: *You* pray and listen, Miss Sister-Keeper. Janet's thirty-three years old, and she acts like she's three. For the life of me, I can't see what your brother Hubert sees in her.

Mercedes (*throwing up her hands in exasperation*): Well, I can. And I will pray and listen for what God wants me to do to help her. Hubert is crazy about her. Been friends with her for a long time.

Tanya: So why doesn't he help her?

Mercedes: Who's to say? (*She pauses, thinking.*) I–I–I don't know. But I think he knows what he's doing and one of these days Janet's going to be my sister!

Tanya: Dreamer!

Mercedes: But listen, let me tell you something about Janet. I saw her in Stop and Shop the other day—she didn't see me—and you know what she did?

Tanya: What?

Mercedes: Well, an old man in front of her at the register tripped and his basket of groceries went flying. Janet got down on her knees to help him!

Tanya: She was probably just looking at the man—ain't even thinking about his groceries. You think she's so in love with your brother Hubert. But you don't know the half. She's man crazy!

Mercedes (*rising, shocked*): I don't *believe* you!

Tanya: Well, maybe she was just being nice for once, but *anybody* would have helped an old man.

Mercedes: Maybe, maybe not. But in this case, it was *Janet* who did.

Tanya: Yeah!

Mercedes (*sitting back down and pointing her finger at Tanya*): Another thing my mother used to say is, "Evil enters like a needle and spreads like an oak tree." You keep thinking badly about Janet, the old devil will have his way with you too. Why are you so bitter, anyway?

Tanya: I'm not bitter. I just call it as I see it. (*Pointedly*) And please get your finger out of my face! Besides, I like most people. It's just that people like Janet *get on my nerves!*

Mercedes (*leaning over toward and gesturing with her hand, eager to get her point across*): The Bible says that we should love our neighbors as ourselves. Think about it. God loves you, and if you love God, how can you hate Janet?

Tanya (*waving her hands at Mercedes*): All right, already. Stop your preaching. I'm not the worst person in the world just because I don't like Janet. And you're not the best because you do.

Mercedes: Oh, I know I've got a lot of negative stuff going on inside me. I've got a lot to work on. And *(reaching over to pat Tanya's hand)* you know what? I'm so glad we're friends. 'Cause you accept me just as I am!

Tanya: So what do you think I should do about Janet?

Mercedes: Pray for her and for yourself. Ask God to renew your mind and help you see Janet in His light!

Tanya: I guess I can do that!

Mercedes: I know you can!

(They get up, fall into playful laughter, and hug each other as the doorbell rings and Margaret Birdy enters from the wings, stage left.)

Mercedes: Oh hi, Margaret. What brings you over this way?

Margaret: I got mixed up on the time. I thought it was five o'clock and it's only four. I was supposed to meet Betty at the bus stop near your house at five. We're going downtown for a light supper and an early movie. I was hoping you wouldn't mind my resting my feet. There's no bench at the bus stop.

Mercedes: Of course not. Come on in. *(Introducing)* This is my friend Tanya. We were just chewing the fat.

Tanya: Hello.

Margaret: Nice to meet you.

Mercedes (*addressing Margaret*): This Betty you're waiting for, is she the one from Connecticut I've heard you talk about?

Margaret: Yes. (*shaking her head*) My good friend Betty. Even though none of her family lives here anymore, she likes to come home for a visit every once in a while.

Tanya (*to Mercedes*): Maybe Margaret's being a sister-keeper by making herself available every time her friend wants to visit.

Margaret: A what?

Mercedes (*laughing*): Sister keeper. I guess that's a new name for me. I'll tell you why one of these days when you have more time.

Margaret: But about Betty. I really am concerned about her. She seems so fragile now. Oh well, that's even more talk for another time!

Tanya: Sometimes I think that all people are interested in is talking about what's wrong in their lives. And if they're divorced or widowed, all they think about is getting another man!

Mercedes (*looking annoyed with Tanya, but speaking to Margaret*): Pay my friend here no mind, Margaret. She's *sweet*, but she likes to pick at folks! (*Then to Tanya*) Margaret's got a husband who supports her all the way. I really do love that man of grace!

Margaret: I can see you two are really buddy-buddies!

Mercedes and Tanya together: We really are! Honest!

Tanya (*looking ashamed*): Margaret, hello. I'm glad to meet you, and I'm glad you found your "man of grace."

Margaret (*reaching over to take Tanya's hand*): Thank you. I'm glad to meet you, too. Any friend of Mercedes is a friend of mine. (*Then to Mercedes*) Well, I guess I'd better start walking back to the bus stop. I'll just use your bathroom before I go, Mercedes. No need to let me out. See you both!

(*As Margaret departs stage left, Mrs. Hope starts walking in from left wing as if about to ring the bell, lightly bumping into each other.*)

Mrs. Hope: (*to Margaret*) Hello. (*Mercedes goes toward the door. Mrs. Hope speaks to Mercedes*) Hi, Mercedes. Was in the neighborhood so thought I'd ring your bell. Hope you don't mind. Busy?

Mercedes: Of course, I don't mind, Mrs. Hope. Come on in. I'm always glad to see you. (*Turning to Tanya and introducing Mrs. Hope*) Tanya, this is Mrs. Elaine Hope. Mrs. Hope, this is my friend Tanya. You've heard me speak of her.

Tanya (*rising*): Hello, Mrs. Hope.

Mrs. Hope: (*noticing an awkward silence*) Am I interrupting something?

Tanya: Oh no--no, you're not. Have a seat. (*Mrs. Hope sits down.*) We were just talking about an old friend who's having some problems. Mercedes thinks we ought to try to help her. (*As she says this, she starts to stage right to fix some tea.*)

Mrs. Hope: That sounds like an OK idea to me.

Tanya: (*Speaking from stage right*) Would you like some tea, Mrs. Hope?

Mrs. Hope: Thank you, Tanya.

Mercedes: (*to Mrs. Hope*) About helping our friend, it's easier said than done. The lady in question is not receptive to me or anyone else right now. It's kind of hard to think of what to say to her.

Mrs. Hope: Well, maybe I could help. I never have much trouble saying anything I want to, Mercedes. Comes with the territory of being old, I guess. (*They laugh.*) And it would be nice to talk to a young person anyway. I'm getting so I don't want to talk to folks my age much. They call me and I just don't feel like talking to them.

Tanya (*coming in with the tea*): All due respect, Mrs. Hope, but that doesn't sound fair. They took the time to call you. Means they're thinking about you!

Mercedes: Forgive her, Mrs. Hope. She's at the beginning of the stage that says, "Have a thought, let it out!"

Mrs. Hope: It's okay. Woman after my own heart! But thinking about me? I don't think so. I think maybe they're so angry about not feeling well that all they want is someone to listen to their ailments: bubbles in the ear, knees wobbling, and they're all as forgetful as I am.

Tanya: I can see why that would be a pain, Mrs. Hope. But …

Mrs. Hope (*interrupting*): And they're mean too. Say something that doesn't suit them and they want to bite your head off. It's just too much trouble dealing with 'em.

Tanya (*thoughtful now*): Mrs. Hope, I sure do think that folks should be able to deal and not take things out on other people, but—well … maybe it's different when you're getting older. Maybe your friends are just lonely and a little tried in their loneliness. Do they have husbands or kids around to talk to?

Mrs. Hope: No. They're really alone.

Mercedes: Tanya's onto something! Maybe they're just extremely lonely and bitter. Remember the story in the book of Ruth? Naomi, Ruth's mother-in-law, was always a pleasant woman, but she turned bitter after she had lost her husband and her sons. She even wanted to be called by another name—Mara, meaning Madam Bitter!

Mrs. Hope: I do remember that story. But Naomi was lucky. Her daughter-in-law Ruth really loved her, didn't she? (*The young women are thoughtful and gaze at Mrs. Hope, as she nods and continues speaking.*) I hadn't really thought of that. My husband died right after we were married, and I never had any kids. Been by myself all my life making do. I guess you can't be lonely for what you never had. (*Turning sideways, patting herself on the knee, and grimacing.*) I guess I'm just a wee bit selfish.

Mercedes: Can't we all be selfish sometimes—and most of the time we don't even realize it. "Have mercy on me, O God, according to your unfailing love—wash away all my iniquity and cleanse me from my sin." Psalm 51 is what comes to my mind when I realize my selfishness!

Tanya (*putting her head down sadly, then speaking to Mrs. Hope*): I don't often *feel* that I'm being selfish, but now that we're talking, I guess I'll have to admit that I am. (*Pauses as if remembering something*) When I was little, my grandmother used to talk to me a lot. She'd read me Bible stories and tell me about her days on the farm. I never, ever grew tired of anything she said. But she's in a nursing home now—has Alzheimer's, and I just can't stand to see her like that. So I never visit.

Mrs. Hope: You never do?

Tanya: I never do.

Mrs. Hope (*opening her bag, getting her calendar, flipping through it, then saying*): I could go to the nursing home with you after you get home on Monday, day after tomorrow, if you'd like.

Tanya (*crying*): Oh, Mrs. Hope, would you?

Mrs. Hope (*smiling*): I would and I will, but it will cost you.

Tanya (*looking at her quizzically through tears*): Carfare?

Mrs. Hope (*gesturing and smiling*): No. Just time. I'd like you to go with me next Saturday to visit my friend Jane. She'll tell us a story or two, I'm sure.

Tanya (*still wiping her eyes, but laughing now*): Oh Mrs. Hope, you are just too much! (*Pausing*) But you know what? Let's not stop with Jane. Maybe you and I could visit other folks once a week—starting with *your* friends! I'm too young to have any but Mercedes—just kidding!

Mrs. Hope: What a wonderful idea! And I know they'd love *you*! Do them good to have a fresh young person around.

Mercedes: Fresh? You got that part right, Mrs. Hope! (*All laugh.*) Say, you two could call yourselves the Dorcas team—you know after that woman in the early church who was always helping everybody. We read about her when we were studying the book of Acts, remember?

Tanya: I don't think we should call ourselves anything. People sometimes shy away when they feel you're pushing Bible down their throats, you know. We'll just be Elaine Hope and Tanya Lothrop coming to visit just because we want to.

Mrs. Hope: Yes!

(*A frantic ringing of the doorbell occurs, Mercedes and Tanya react; Mercedes goes to open the door, stage left.*)

Kim (*out of breath*): Mercedes, is Hubert here with you guys? We got a crisis in the family! Mom wants Hubert to come over and put a new bulb in the bathroom ceiling. Janet's been out forever, and Mom doesn't want me to get on a ladder!

Mercedes: No, Kim. Hubert's not here right now. But I'll go over and change the bulb for your mother. (*To Tanya and Margaret*) I'll be right back. (*Speaking to Kim as they head for the door, stage left*) Why don't you come over some Saturday, Kim? Tell me what's going on with you. Give me some pointers on teenage life. Might have to use them some day.

Kim (*laughing*): Life? What kind of life do I have? (*Thoughtfully and pointedly*) I've got two mothers—Janet and Mom. And they are *ex-treme*! Don't do this, do that! Go here, go there—forever and ever Amen! I wish Janet would act like she's my *sister*! She's *not my mom*! (*Mercedes and Kim go offstage left.*)

Tanya: Mrs. Hope, you know what I think just happened here?

Mrs. Hope: What?

Tanya: We had a *wow* moment!

Mrs. Hope: Hmm—what's a *wow* moment?

Tanya: You talk to someone for a minute and *wow*, things just start falling into place.

Mrs. Hope: As in?

Tanya: Well, Mercedes and I were here talking about being a sister to a friend. And we did not agree about that at all, at all! And then we had three quick visitors who had their own things going on.

Mrs. Hope: Yes—

Tanya: And we found out that we had some stuff going on too.

Mrs. Hope: Uh-huh …

Tanya: And then it seemed that we were really listening to each other!

Mrs. Hope: You know, in Ecclesiastes somewhere it says: "Two are better than one: because they have a good reward for their work and they gain a lot just because they stick together"—something like that!

Tanya: Something like that. Yes, that makes sense. And you know, I was kind of teasing Mercedes with a name, *sister keeper,* and now I think that name applies to me as well, and you, and Margaret, and even Kimberly—although she doesn't know it yet. We've all gotta be sister-keepers. *Super* sister *keepers*!

Mrs. Hope: Here's where I get to say *wow*!

(Tanya and Mrs. Hope get up, put their arms around each other, and walk offstage.)

Epilogue

When players return for a bow, they join hands in a line swaying as they sing verse 1 of "Blest Be the Tie that Binds." After singing the first verse, they invite the congregation to join them on the remaining verses.

Blest be the tie that binds
Our hearts in Christian love
The fellowship of kindred minds
Is like to that above.

Before our Father's throne
We pour our ardent prayers,
Our fears, our hopes, our aims are one--
Our comforts and our cares.

We share each other's woes,
Each other's burdens bear
And often for each other flows
The sympathizing tear.

From sorrow, toil, and pain,
And sin we shall be free;
And perfect love and joy shall reign
Through all eternity.

"Blest Be the Tie That Binds"
Public Domain

Sometimes there's nothing to say. This is one of those times. The story "It Should Have Been Me" and the essay "Fine but Sad" that follow were painful to write, but I wrote them anyway.

~

It Should Have Been Me!

"The Lord giveth and the Lord taketh away. Blessed be the name of the Lord," the venerable Reverend Dr. Holyfield Copher intoned, closing the funeral service. His black bowler glistened in the light rain. Gertrude Haynes Johnson, my wife of thirty-three years was dead. "Oh God," I groaned, falling to my knees on the soggy green carpet.

"It should have been me. I'm ninety years old and ready to die, but Truda—only sixty-nine. It's too soon, too soon! It should have been me!"

As people headed for their cars, the saxophonist played the grand old rag "When the Saints Go Marching In." I could almost hear Gertrude's off-key soprano shrilling the words: *Lord, I want to be in that number when the saints go marching' in!*

"You will be in that number, dear," I whispered to her silent ears. My mind raced back to the day she had died.

"Bertram," she had called from the bathroom. Her voice was raspy, soft. "Bert—help me!" I'd shoved open the bathroom door and found her sitting, her neck limp, sweat rolling down her face.

"It'll be all right, Truda," I'd said. My heart was a relentless drumbeat as I lifted her and placed her on the bed. "Just lie still, honey. I'm calling an ambulance."

Her eyes opened just a little. They were dull yellow, not Truda's eyes. "No hospital," she'd said. "No hospital." And then nothing—forever!

Now, as the funeral director helped me into the family car, a soft touch on my shoulder brought me back to the present. Before I could turn to acknowledge it, an unfamiliar voice said, "I'm Neesha, Pops."

Neesha? It was Tanecia, Gertrude's youngest granddaughter. The last time I'd seen her she was ten years old, but I recognized her still. She was her grandma all over. Same yellow-toned skin and high cheekbones, same tight-lipped half smile. Same oak colored hair, only hers fell loosely to her shoulder. Truda's had been short and kinky.

"I'm sorry, Pops," she murmured. "Real sorry." She slipped a piece of paper into my pocket and was gone.

A deep hurt about Neesha had raged inside Gertrude. Neesha—she'd have to be about twenty-seven now—had run away when she was fourteen, and about a year later, her mother, Pansy, Gertrude's only daughter, hanged herself. Gertrude had blamed Neesha. I'd tried to remind her of Pansy's instability long before Neesha's folly, but she'd always said, "No, it was Neesha. Broke her mother's heart, she did."

After the service, a few folks came by. I didn't feel much like company, but Gertrude would have liked showing off our *blessed condo*, as she'd called it. When they left, I told Gertrude all about the funeral "… And Neesha came, Truda. I don't know where she came from—didn't say, but she gave me her phone number. Should I call her?"

Weeks limped into months, and my old shoe of a chair sagged under the day and night assault of my weight. Gertrude's cross-stitch wall hangings grew soft beards of dust, and tarnish rested moodily on the table beneath the oversized picture of Gertrude and me.

Seven months of hermit living discouraged my friends from coming by, or even calling. Then one day, the doorbell rang. Who in the world could it be? Pastor Copher had come a few times in the early months, but he had long stopped trying to cheer me.

Three blind mice, three blind mice, the bell sang again. I smiled. Years ago when we bought that bell, Gertrude had said, "That crazy Three Blind Mice tune will bless our marriage by making us smile."

At the time I'd pooh-poohed it, saying, "That's about a wife cutting off mouse tails. Why would I smile?"

Truda did her little neck and shoulder thing, shrugging her shoulders and twisting her neck, as if to say, "You will 'cause I say so!"

The bell rang again, insistently this time, and I shook away my memories. I pressed the intercom. It was Neesha. "Hi, Pops," she stuttered, as she walked in the door. When I saw her the day of the funeral, Neesha seemed tall, almost stately, but today she was small and disheveled, her coat missing a button, her hair straggly. "You gotta help me Pops," she said, brushing away a tear. "I don't know where else to turn."

"Neesha," I began. "I—"

"I lost my job, Pops. And I had a big fight with the quote unquote friend I was staying with. She pushed me so hard I fell into the bushes by the house. Ain't that nothin'?"

Tanecia did the same saucy neck and shoulder thing I thought belonged only to her grandmother.

"Can I stay here with you—please, Pops? I could be a big help. I can cook, and I'd wash your clothes—and ..."

I flushed. The thought was distasteful. "Neesha, your grandma blamed you for your momma's death. I don't think she'd want you staying here. But ..." I reached for my wallet. "I want to help." Neesha shook her head, and her tears fell swiftly.

Oh God, how can I handle this? "Neesha," I said. "There's another thing. You know how people are. What would they think? You, such a young girl, staying alone with an old man."

"But Pops, you're my grandpa; you were married to Gramma. Don't that make you my grandpa?"

"It would if we'd had that family kind of relationship, but we didn't, Tanecia. You know that. You and I are practically strangers."

"No—please Pops—Grandpa?"

I couldn't answer. Truth was, I was a little scared of Neesha. Truda had always called her "just plain evil." *Suppose she hurt me—I am an old man!*

"Pops," Neesha interrupted. "Tell you what. Just let me stay tonight. In the morning I'll find a shelter; I promise."

I felt blood drain from my face. "All right, Neesha, just tonight. I'll call around tomorrow and help you find someplace."

"Thanks, Pops." Neesha lowered her eyes and looked ten years old again. I wanted to take her in my arms and hold her, but I didn't.

Sunlight urged me awake the next day, and as I rolled away from morning stiffness and reached for my cane, I thought about the inevitability of pain—mine, Truda's, Neesha's. When Neesha came out of the bathroom, I beckoned to her to sit with me on the lumpy brown sofa that shifted every which way on its own.

"Neesha," I began. "We got a problem, but this old man knows something about being young and goin' wrong for a while. So let's look at three months. You look for a job every day, and when you get one, start looking for a room. Meantime, you can help me keep this place up. Between my stomach and old Mr. Arthur Rytis, I ain't moving as fast as I used to."

Neesha threw her arms around me. Then she pulled back, embarrassed. "Oh Pops, I'm like—I'm like—you won't be sorry!"

I wasn't sorry. Neesha did her share, and her cooking found its way to my heart. "Where'd you learn to cook so good?" I asked her.

"At a shelter. It's like—I got a job there for about six months while I was waiting for my baby, and like, the cook there was a real chef and I helped her a lot."

"You had a baby? You have a child? What? Where?"

She dismissed the barrage with a curt, "A girl, stillborn. I'll tell you about it sometime."

I put off prying, and little by little over the next few months, she told me much about the past thirteen years and before. She wanted to hear from me as well. "Tell me about you and Gramma," she'd say. "Did you know her first husband? Tell me about momma and the other kids."

"Want to play a game?" I asked her one evening.

"Yeah, what?"

"High achiever. It's a card game about stuff most people don't know about us black folks."

"I'd love that, Pops," she said. "You know Gramma read me all kinds of black history when I was little—Harriet Tubman and the Underground Railroad, Frederick Douglas. She even gave me a real old poetry book by Paul Laurence Dunbar. It was like I learned to read by that book! Gramma read the poems over and over."

"Yes, your grandma really loved Dunbar. *Grandma's gone a visitin', seen her get her shawl…*" I recited.

"When I was a-hidin' there 'hind the garden wall." Neesha finished the line. "It's called 'Opportunity,' about a kid who thought he was fooling his grandma and she had him all figured out!

"I'll read some Dunbar to you, Pops. I love the dialect," she said. "That is, if I can ever get my stuff from that thing I used to live with.

I've like, called her so many times, but she won't answer the phone. I'm scared to go over there, 'cause I don't know what she might do. She and her boyfriend pulled a knife on me once."

I winced. "Best you stay away from her, Neesha. Just let the things go!"

Three months was almost up, and Neesha hadn't found a job, but neither of us spoke of it. By now, I was more concerned about what was going on with her. Did she have friends other than the housemate?

"Why don't you invite a friend over once in a while?" I offered one day. She shrugged. Still, no one called or came, so I was surprised to be awakened one midnight by loud voices from the living room. I pulled on my robe and shuffled to the door.

"Oh, hi, Pops," a young woman with a drink in her hand shouted. "We making too much noise?"

Another young woman and a guy sat together in my old chair, oblivious to my presence, a spilled bottle on the floor beside them. Neesha stared at me, her mouth open as she stood by the patio doors. "Pops," she started.

"Get out, get out, get out! All of you!" I didn't know I could yell so loud!

The revelers flew, Neesha with them. "In your room, girl," I shouted grabbing and pulling her back. In the morning, I lectured big time! She listened unresponsively, and for about three weeks, she chilled me with politeness. My attempts to blanket the chill brought courteous rebuffs. "Neesha, honey, let's play High Achiever," I'd say.

"Too tired, thank you, Pops," she'd respond.

Or, "How's about going to church with me Sunday? There's a dynamite young preacher in town. Hear he's bringing in young people like crazy!"

"Another time, thank you, Pops."

After a while, the ice thawed, and our talks grew stronger than ever, but one evening, I sensed she wanted no talk from me. She kept glancing at the clock, and during supper, she only picked at her food. "Something troubling you, child?" I asked.

"No, Pops, no. Only I was like—wondering—can I borrow Gramma's car tonight? A new friend—she's nice—asked me to meet her at the movies and those buses are so slow. Just this once, please, Pops."

In its lifetime, Gertrude's thirteen-year-old car had never been driven by anyone but Gertrude, and I intended to hold to that. Suddenly, I heard Gertrude's voice as clearly as if she were standing beside me, "Oh, I give up, Bert. Let the child use the car—and Bert—tell her I forgive her!"

"Okay, Neesha," I said. "I guess your grandmother wouldn't mind—but be real careful. She was awful persnickety about that car!"

"Grandpa, I mean Pops, I know all about cars. I've had two!" Her impish grin replaced the restlessness I'd sensed earlier and settled me.

"*Grandpa* is okay, Neesha," I said. "Enjoy the movie."

Around one in the morning, the phone booted me awake. *Don't Neesha hear that phone?* I picked it up, intending to give a piece of my mind.

"Bertram Johnson," the voice on the other end rasped. "This is the police. You know a Tanecia Mills? She's down here at station five. Picked her up with a guy we've been watching—a salesman—if you know what I mean. She gave us your phone number. Said you were her grandfather. Can you come down here?"

I couldn't believe my eyes when I saw her. Hers were glazed over, and her clothes reeked of liquor.

"Pops, please," she said. "It's not my fault. I used to kind of like him, and I thought he liked me. I did not know he was a pusher, honest, Pops. We were in this bar, and he held my mouth open and poured a drink down my throat. Then he smashed the bottle, and it went all over me. Because I wouldn't do drugs with him. I wouldn't, you know, Pops. I don't do that no more, and I don't drink."

"Any charges against her?" I asked the officer.

"Just the charge of keeping bad company, Mr. Johnson. You can take her home, but you may want to take her to a hospital. She seems okay now, but she was talking real crazy a while ago. I'll drive you; we've got to keep the car a couple of days."

"She'll be all right, officer," I said. "We'll go home. She doesn't need a hospital. I believe her, and I believe in her. You won't see her down here again. Neesha, come on, girl."

Her body was heavy with sleep as I got her out of the car, to her feet, into the elevator, and into bed. I lay awake all night. By nine the next morning, Neesha hadn't stirred, making me wonder if she really had been drinking last night and was sleeping off a hangover.

It was about ten, but hangover or no hangover, we were going to have to talk! I knocked on the door, my speech prepared: *Neesha, it's like you're blind and letting something bad lead you. God's been leading me all these years, and if you let Him, He'll lead you too. Trust me, please, Neesha. I want to help you. You've brought joy to my life in such a short time!* Silence answered my knock.

"Neesha dear, come on, get up. I know things are bothering you, but we can handle it. Come on, get up!"

I waited a few minutes, knocked again, and pushed the door open. Striding over to shake her awake, I gasped. A bottle—the pills my dentist had prescribed when she pulled my tooth last month—was on its side on the night table—empty. A piece of paper torn out of a notebook lay crumpled on the floor. I picked it up. The scribble was hardly legible, but I made it out—*granpa im sorry*

I felt her pulse. My cold, bony fingers dialed 911. "Come," I said in a voice that was not my own. "My granddaughter is dead."

Fine, but Sad

Each creak of the old rocker punctuates Juliet Jones's mood—thoughts of the years that have passed, some too quickly, others not quickly enough—decades folding into decades. An especially loud series of creaks proclaims her future: *life-closes-not-with-a bang-but-a-whimper!*

A financially comfortable, personable, active "senior citizen" in her fourth year of retirement, Juliet wonders, *Is this all?*

People from many corners have touched Juliet's life. She has a couple of close friends; the fences that she had any part in breaking have been mended. Her marriage, though ended, resulted in a wonderful son to carry on a family name. A devout Christian, Juliet has lived her faith as well as she can. Her prayer life is dutiful, and she is sensitive to the needs of others. She has watched sunsets and sun risings and been awed by their beauty. Nevertheless, as she reflects, Juliet Jones confides to an absent audience that not now, not ever has she had zest for life. "I'm fine, but sad," she says.

In ancient Greece, a physician named Hippocrates set forth the notion that the way a person views life, the way that person feels, is governed by his/her personality type. Much later, a psychologist in Germany and one in the United States said, "No, it's their body build that determines the way people feel and act." Still another philosopher put everyone in two boxes—introvert and extrovert. Skeptics tossed out the idea of studying feelings altogether. And round and round, round and round! Is the controversy still raging, or has it been settled once and for all? Juliet Jones would like to know.

When Juliet dares to confess her feelings to her friends, their mouths fall open. "I don't see why you feel that way, Julie," one tells her. "You have so much to live for. I know your knees give you a fit, but that's life. We all have that! And look, you don't owe anybody anything, your house is all paid for, you've got so many good friends! And what about your son Jimmy, the best plumber in town, expecting your first grandchild?"

"Go to the doctor!" says another. "Get some exercise!" How many times has Juliet heard that? "You're just feeling sorry for yourself," another boldly speaks. "Get involved!"

On occasion, Juliet has tried to share her feelings with her pastor. But somehow whenever she talks to him, she feels no personal contact. "God loves you, Mrs. Jones," he'll say. "Just continue studying His word, keep praying, He'll lift you up. Remember, God loves you!" Juliet guesses that her understanding of God's love falls short of that of her pastor.

Juliet doesn't need to see a doctor. She visits an internist faithfully every year. "For a person your age," the doctor has said, "you're in excellent shape. Just try to lose a few pounds. That will help your arthritis pain; you'll soon be feeling right up to speed!"

Therapy? Twenty years ago, Juliet visited a psychotherapist about a problem she was having with her son. The problem was soon resolved, but Juliet stayed on, *entertaining myself,* as she put it. *It was like being on vacation, relaxing with a friend. I hated when he looked at his watch to end the fifty-minute hour. I hated it, too, when the therapist ruled me cured. No need to try that again!*

Juliet exercises a little—not formally. She admits to being lazy in that regard. Still she moves about a lot, and she's by no means a couch potato. When she was younger, she used to walk miles enjoying the countryside. Now she walks miles—albeit stop-and-go miles—in all the city malls! She can't get any busier! Although she has pain in her back and knees, she transports patients at a hospital for a couple of hours a week on Mondays, tutors a small group of children at church on Tuesday mornings, and studies art at the local art center in the afternoon. On Wednesdays she goes to a mall. On Thursdays, she does housework. On Fridays, it's back to the mall— to return most of the things she bought a week ago Wednesday!

Juliet subscribes to a couple of devotional magazines and reads them cover-to-cover as soon as they arrive. In the wee hours of the morning, when she awakes from her erratic sleep, she snatches a chapter or two from the Christian novels she keeps by her bedside. *I need constant reassurance that life is worth it,* she says wryly.

And yes, she does feel ashamed, particularly as she reads stories that tell of people overcoming problems far worse than any she's encountered. She's aware that even people she knows might long to trade places with her. But despite her awareness and her shame, there is no doubt in Juliet's mind that she has walked, is walking, and will continue to walk a lonely, unfulfilled mile.

Is Juliet Jones simply a self-centered person questing an impossible dream? Is Juliet Jones someone whose efforts to be perfect have produced self-hatred— anger with herself because she never dared to accept her imperfections and roll with them? Is Juliet Jones a victim of predetermined melancholy?

Innumerable theories, both secular and religious, have been set forth; endless treatments have been proposed by those seeking to explain and support the feelings and strivings of human beings. But when it comes right down to it, does anyone really know why one person acts and enjoys while another reacts, endures, and accepts or why still another, like Juliet, lives fully, but only in the eyes of the beholder!

Learning to Live;
Living to Learn

I belong to a group of seniors who call ourselves *the Swingers*. They asked me to write a play for them, and I responded by having them fill out a questionnaire to tell me a little about their years growing up. We are a diversified group, some have lived much of their lives in the southern states of the United States; others grew up in the northern states. Still others grew up abroad. Scene 3, quoted here, of the longer play (*Our Times Are in His Hands*) is a summation of what they shared with me.

I'm Swinger Hester Histry, and
I'll just sit here for a while
And tell you things about us,
Some of which may make you smile.

And some may make you think about
Your own lives—how they're going,
And cause you to reflect
On things that you've been knowing
Need changing!

We did not always understand
That *our times were in **His** hands*
Or that the times when we fell down
Were preparation for our crowns—
But today we bow in praise
For the wonder God has made
Of our lives!

In the South and in the North
And even across the seas,
We found ourselves at various schools
Learning to live with ease.

In the North *these* bid us come
Take of learning's store:
Roxbury Memorial, Practical Arts,
Girls High School, and more—

Hampton Institute, Booker T. High,
And others too numerous to name—
Fed our brains while as down South,
We prepared to claim our fame!

Enfield, Middlesex in England,
Across the ocean blue—
Another stop along the way
To doing what we do!

Some subjects were a challenge,
But we learned them well;
Graduation days soon came,
And we were feeling swell!

(*Swell was our word back then.
Do you hear me? Can you say amen?*)

We wore bobby socks and pressed our hair
With straightening combs on the stove.
Sometimes we did that every day
To keep the kinks on hold!

We wore our first three-inch heels—
No mean feat way back then.

We learned to dance and flirt with boys
As they strove to be men!

There were historic moments too
That we knew of firsthand:
Joe Louis won the title;
Duke Ellington had a band;
Jackie Robinson, baseball's star,
Showed guts that he was made of;
President Roosevelt served our land
For three terms—now unheard of!

We worked in factories, cleaned people's homes,
Had Thursdays off and all—
And on the weekends did our thing—
We really had a ball!

And while we were out there living,
New things came into view;
Our futures were ahead of us—
What could we hope to do
To fill the distant yearnings
Of our restless selves to rise
Somewhere above the ordinary?
Somewhere nearer stars and sky?

One dreamed of becoming a pilot,
Of flying a jet plane,
But motherhood's joys came first in her life,
And she piloted the home team's train!

Becoming a poet was another's dream:
That dream has now come true.
This lady delights us all the time

With a lofty verse or two!

Another dreamed of midwifery—
A challenge to obtain,
But with family's help, she made it—
And that was society's gain!

And sometimes sickness challenged us—
Perhaps polio the worst;
The pains were great, the medicines few,
But we were not the first
To learn that way to stand up tall
Against all pain and strife,
To learn how not to drop the ball—
To prepare for unfair life!

We got into unheard-of scrapes
And didn't know what to do,
But we managed with ingenuity
To step up and follow through!

Now here's a funny thing one of us did—
Killed a chicken on the floor
and wondered how she'd clean it up
before her ma walked in the door!
Well, here is how she did it—
Plucked the chicken, cooked it too,
And ate it all by Ma's returrn—
Do you think that was easy to do?

Our parents raised us strictly,
Whipped us when we were wrong;
And though we stormed, we loved them still.
They taught us to be strong!

And then one day, the testing came.
Now we were parents too—
The times had changed, we had to choose
To do or not to do
What our well-meaning folks had taught us.
Were they way behind the times?
Or as some people put it,
        Was there gold in them there mines?

Some of us wouldn't change a thing,
And some would change it all.
For that's the way life is, you know
It's every person's call.

And some of our parents never said a word
About true love and sex,
So ignorance sometimes brought us
Pain from one generation to the next.

We vowed we'd save our children
By listening intently to their woes:
We'd talk of everything we knew,
Look largely at the current stew,
And help them come to see God's clue
About it!

Ours were the baby boomers
Whom you hear about today,
And most of them have made top news
In the game of life they play!

But some of them have not, you know—
Fallout has come to bear.
We'd like to tell you those stories

But we can't—too much pain to share!

We taught our *own* and sometimes more;
That was the way back then.
If children needed someone,
We were quick to take them in.

We learned to trust, and not to trust—
Looked at one hand then the other
To decide if the left hand needed to know
That the right hand was its brother!

We hoped if we were trustworthy
That others would be too.
Oh yes, that's what we *hoped* for
And *sometimes* it came true.

We asked for help from others.
It came often, often not.
We learned not to be surprised
When what we hoped for was *not* what we got!

Sometimes, oh yes, we had to deal
With husbands who had strayed.
God said forgive and try again;
Not all of of us obeyed!

And, too, we lost *dear* husbands
To death's hard, icy hand.
But we had hope in what Jesus said
About the Promised Land!

He said we'd get to heaven,
See friends and family,
And live with Him forever

Throughout eternity!

We learned that families stood by us
When death and sorrow came;
We learned to focus on God's love
Through folks who shared our pain.

We learned from the devotions
Conducted in our homes.
We learned to pray in simple ways
As each child prayed on his own!

Sometimes we wondered, "Where is God?"
He seemed so far away—
But experience proved Him nearer
As we served Him day by day.

We lived through wars—a few of them.
Our brothers, they did too
With no complaint of injustice felt
As they served red, white, and blue.

We worry about society
Especially today,
We can't do much about it,
But we constantly pray—

About its seeming lack of conscience.
Its selfishness supreme,
Its ruthlessness, ungodliness,
Its failings scene by scene by scene.

Still, we vote in today's elections,
Trying to get what community needs;
We work as voter registrars,

Encouraging nonvoters to speed
Up!

In fact, you'll see us in many a place
Volunteering our expertise
And thanking God for days well spent
With the gift of His increase!

We pray that as the Bible says
He'll hear and heal our land;
We pray that those who hear *us*
Will also hear what *He* commands.

For we believe He's calling us
To get hearts right with Him;
Not just our own, but others too—
This world is growing dim.

We go to many funerals
And share the bulletins,
Rejoicing in wonderful memories
Of our old childhood friends.

We tell each other of aches and pains,
Comparing all the while,
And close each conversation
With somewhat of a smile.

For we're all in this together,
Living out the fullness of our time,
And we go each day to the garden
Praying "not my will, but Thine!"

Choir sings "In the Garden"
I come to the garden alone,

While the dew is still on the roses;
And the voice I hear,
Falling on my ear,
The Son of God discloses.

Refrain
And He walks with me,
And He talks with me,
And he tells me I am His own,
And the joy we share
As we tarry there,
None other has ever known.

He speaks and the sound of His voice
Is so sweet, the birds hush their singing;
And the melody that He gave to me
Within my heart is ringing.

Refrain

I'd stay in the garden with Him
Tho' the night around me be falling;
But He bids me go
Through the voice of woe,
His voice to me is calling.

Refrain

"In the Garden"
Public Domain

We Swingers meet on Tuesdays at 11:00 and get involved in all manner of things. We eat lavishly and try to make it right by doing exercises led by one of our members. Community speakers come to discuss important topics—health care, housing, etc. Once we were told about a competition in creativity that was being held just for seniors. Some of us entered and had a grand old time performing a Paul Laurence Dunbar poem—Guess what? We won the competition!

Conversation

Literally this is the last poem I put to paper, but I have rewritten it many times in the last few years. It keeps coming back to me for change, but it doesn't change much. I've had my conversations— and I think I've found my symphony! I dedicate this poem to my fourteen-year-old great-grandniece April Alderete, who is already beginning to find hers!

Friend, I heard you singing—
May I have a copy of your song?
I'd really like to sing along.
It sounds so sweet, the words, the beat—
All make me feel that I belong!

What's that you say, "Go write my own"?
Would that I could!
My fingers should be made of wood
For all of their creating!

Oh, not from fingers comes a song?
From where, then?
From a soul, a heart, a mind?
From unique joys and sorrows?
And anyone can find his song?

Then I'll find mine—
The song of my life's joy and pain,
The song I've lived so long to gain;
And I will seek the best of others' songs
With which to empathize,

With which to harmonize,
With which to win, perchance, the prize—

A symphony?

Yes!

Acknowledgments

Special thanks to all who contributed to this work of many years.

Thank you, Mom and Dad, who praised every pencil stroke I made as a child.

Many thanks, Debra Kruk and Gwen Lewis, for urging me to publish

Thank you John, Helen, Edgar. Bill and all your offspring for making me matriarch of our family

Thank you, Dr. Estelle J. Clasing, Rev. Marilyn Becker, and the congregation of the Grace and Hope Mission, Boston, for making it possible for my *very first* play (and several others) to be presented to our community at large.

Thank you to The Swingers Fellowship of Twelfth Baptist Church who inspired the play *Our Times Are in His Hands*, and who shared so much love and faith with us all at our meetings led by Frances Sims and Grace Locker,

Bless you, Nichola Whitehorn for sharing with me your "God-inspired" vision to create a "ministry of love for the Women's Fellowship of Twelfth Baptist Church.

Special thanks to Dr. Charmaine Martin, Martine Cadet , Professor Veronica Ellis, Roberta Jarrett and Sister Rose Marie Cummins, who graciously worked with me as they read part or all of the fledgling manuscript

Many thanks, Leola Phillips, my birthday twin, for "standing by"

For the prayers lifted up on behalf of each member by our Monday night Bible Study Group, thank you Rev. Paula Waters.

As Tiny Tim, my favorite book character, would say, "God bless us everyone!